PORTMADOC

AND ITS RESOURCES 1856

BY

MADOG AP OWAIN GWYNEDD

Edited by Richard Walwyn

EDITOR'S INTRODUCTION

This book about Porthmadog was written and published in English in 1856 in the form of an essay for an unspecified historical or literary society, just over thirty years after the town was founded. It is, therefore, one of the earliest accounts we have of its history. It was published in one edition and is now scarce (Gwynedd Library Service has two copies, and the National Library of Wales has another four), so it seemed appropriate to re-issue it in the present form. It has been used as a primary source by many later writers on the history of the area, but has not always been acknowledged.

Madog ap Owain Gwynedd, the bardic name of the author, was the legendary prince who sailed from the area in the 12th century to land and later colonise North America. It has not proved possible to find anything about the author other than that he was probably called Owen Morris.

Some typographical errors in the original have been corrected, but apart from that the document is reproduced as faithfully as possible, including pagination and line breaks; this is a very near facsimile of the 1856 publication.

In the original document the spelling, particularly of place names, followed the practice of the age and a lot of this will jar on the eye of a reader accustomed to current Welsh spelling. However, as this is a historical document, I thought it best to retain the original spelling, so have used Portmadoc rather than Porthmadog and so on.

The early part of the book describes conditions in the area before the arrival on the scene of W A Madocks, and then proceeds to a detailed account of the building of the Cob and the founding of the port and town of Porthmadog. He tells the story of the failed attempt by Madocks and others to make Porth Dinllaen rather than Holyhead the port of departure for Ireland. If the scheme had succeeded this would have radically transformed the development of the area. The early days of the Ffestiniog railway are described, and he writes of the desirability of a main-line connection to England. This did eventually happen, but not until eleven years after the publication of the book.

The author comments on the social conditions of his time and present day inhabitants of Porthmadog may be a little shocked to read about the sorry state of mid-nineteenth century sewage disposal arrangements, and may also be surprised to learn that the houses round Heol y Parc had cellars which were let as very sub-standard housing.

In keeping with the spirit of his times, the author was much concerned with the moral and educational state of his town. On the whole he writes with approval of the facilities being developed and he praises the part played by luminaries such as David Williams of Bron Eryri (later renamed to Castell Deudraeth) and Samuel Holland of Plas Penrhyn, both of whom contributed greatly to the wellbeing of the young town. He praises the sober and orderly behaviour of the "labouring classes" – "here there are no drunken brawls and riots creating disquietude and disorder" – and relates with pride that, despite its size, the neighbourhood has not one police constable.

He describes in some detail the state in 1856 of the various industries on which the town depended for its burgeoning prosperity, particularly shipping, slate mining and quarrying.

Richard Walwyn
Borth-y-Gest
2013

Porthmadog harbour in 1850 from a lithograph by C F Williams

PORTMADOC

And its Resources.

BY

MADOG AP OWAIN GWYNEDD

1856

BLAENAU FESTINIOG :

PRINTED BY JONES AND ROBERTS, HIGH STREET.

PREFACE.

THE author of this composition has to regret the pressure of time, which prevented him from forwarding to the Meeting a *fair* copy of the essay, and which, also, rendered him unable to correct many errors, and supply many deficiencies, which, otherwise, he might have been able to accomplish.

There are some dates wanting:—these the author expected to have found out before the time appointed to send the compositions to the Secretary, but failed in doing so.

CHAPTER I.

PORTMADOC, AND ITS RESOURCES.

––––––––––

WE prefer the vocation of the Chronicler or Contemporary Historian to that of the Antiquary. It has for us a more true and heartfelt interest and a more powerful spell than the other. True, the imagination of the Antiquary is led captive to scenes of past glory and grandeur, by the grey mouldering ruins that surround him. And we can fully appreciate and enter into the blissful feelings that move his breast, when silently communing with the fallen dilapidated column, or the crumbling remains of an arch—which whisper to him of those mighty geniuses who raised to themselves these monuments—of the scenes of triumph, pomp, and revelry that once were seen where silent desolation now sits alone,—of the domestic happiness and social felicity of the inhabitants, or may be of the pain and misery produced by some national disaster or local calamity. But after all, the mind cannot but revert to the fact that there is no immediate connection—no vital principle, existing between it and the ruins that are before it. It cannot but view as strangers the spirits conjured and represented before it by fancy. They are children of other days—having other feelings and associations, and holding no direct relations with the present inhabitants of our world. In this aspect, the labours of the contemporary Historian are decidedly of greater interest and importance than the most successful of Antiquarian researches, inasmuch as the first bear on the affairs, associations and events, and reflect the feelings of the present—which will always transcend over the past, however brilliant may be its story and glorious its annals. A narrative of the rise and progress of Liverpool, Manchester, or London merits more attention from the *generality* of mankind than the history of the decline and fall of Tyre, Carthage, or Nineveh. The first have some relation with the everyday concerns and wellbeing of the humblest cottager, as well as their influence on the prosperity of him who counts his acres by the thousands,—

while the others, save their earnings, claim the study of only the comparative few—the learned and the wealthy.

Viewed as the consummation of the schemes of a far-seeing mind, and as the creation and a result of modern speculative commerce, Portmadoc and its history must present much that is interesting and instructive. Sixty years ago, a traveller passing through the defiles of Snowdon—the scenes of many sanguinary battles between the Welsh and their Saxon invaders—and emerging from the terrific grandeur of the terrific pass of Aberglaslyn, wending his way towards Tanybwlch through Nanmor (when the celebrated poets Dafydd Nanmor, and Rhys Goch Eryri flourished), and along the base of Cnicht and Moelwyn mountains—then the postal route from Caernarvon to Maentwrog, Harlech, and Barmouth,—would have had on his right hand, an estuary of great extent and beauty spread before his view. This estuary was called *Traeth mawr*, and except to the westward, towards Cardigan Bay, was enclosed by mountains and hills. A branch of the Snowdonian range, *Y Foel Ddu*, bounded it on the north side; to the south, a series of headlands, running aslant to its direction, separated it from an adjacent branch of the sea, called *Traeth bach*, and then the proud figure of Snowdon, Cnicht with its sharp peak, and that curiously formed two-headed mountain, Moelwyn, completely sheltered it on its eastern side.

Its greatest length from Pont Aberglaslyn to a place on the Carnarvonshire side—*Trwyn Garth Penyclogwyn*—was about seven miles; its breadth varied—being from the last place named point to Trwynypenrhyn on the opposite side (the extreme point of the intervening land dividing this arm of the sea from the neighbouring one of Traeth bach), only a mile, while it was two and three miles broad at other points in its extent. Dafydd Nanmor wrote the following *englyn* regarding the time of the tide at this place:—

"Yn nydd, y Lloer newydd, ar naw—o'r gloch,
Y gwlych y llanw eithiaw; __
Y llawn ddydd, y llanw a ddaw
I'r nod, lle bu'r newidiaw."

(TRANSLATION).

" At nine o'clock of Luna's change,
'Tis full sea on the shore;
And, on the day that Luna's full,
'Tis full sea the same hour."

At the flow of the tide, when fairly covered by the sea, this estuary exhibited a scene of picturesque beauty, rarely equalled. Numerous little islets, clothed with luxuriant wood and verdure dotted its bosom, while the encompassing mountains cast their shadows on, or were reflected by its smooth, clear mirror. A tiny skiff might have been seen, after warily creeping from behind a projecting headland, and threading its way through the shadows of the Foel Ddu, and Foel Hebog, and amongst the islets—entering into the warm gleam of the sun—its owner and passengers awaking into songs of happiness and bliss, which the surrounding echoes long and faithfully imitated. According to an old tradition, Madog ap Owain Gwynedd set sail from one of these islands on his expedition in search of a new country, and to avoid and escape from the dissensions of his brothers respecting the succession to the throne of their father. It is worthy of note that there were several places to which the name of Madog was attached long before W. A. Madocks, Esq., formed a connection with the neighbourhood, such as Ynysfadog, Brynmadog, &c., which gives a shade of truth to the tradition. At the reflux of the tide, the appearance of this indentation of the sea was far from being of so prepossessing a character. Numerous sandbanks made up the middle of it, through which the Glaslyn river lazily flowed, and which were fringed towards the sides with some coarse unsightly vegetation. Where now—

> "The lowing herd winds slowly o'er the lea,
> The ploughman homeward plods his weary way."

Where now luxuriant crops of grain wave their heavy tops, and numerous herds of cattle browse amidst the plenteous grass—then was a wild uncultivated and uninviting waste: where the cheerful sounds of agricultural avocations, the hum and turmoil of busy trade, and the mirth-creating laugh of boisterous youngsters are now heard—then only resounded with the wild, dismal notes of the curlew in its wheeling flights, and the cries of seabirds proclaiming the glooming loneliness of the surrounding solitude. And the spot on which the pleasant flourishing seaport of Portmadoc stands, with its well-built houses, its harbour full of vessels, and reverberating with the sounds of business, and the clangour of artificers,—was then occupied by bare sandbanks, on which the cormorant perched himself to swallow his catch, and over which the western wave rolled unobstructed.

Although fordable at some points at ebb, it was not without great hazard and peril that a passage could be made across the estuary, as the returning tide sometimes swept in with inconceivable rapidity, and the person crossing found himself in danger of being enclosed by it, and his life thus placed in jeopardy. Great many lives were thus lost from time to time. Many a poor benighted traveller—perhaps returning from his world-wide wanderings to the home of his fathers, found his grave on the dreary sands of Traeth Mawr. Whether such had been the condition of this territory from earliest times, or whether it fell under the dominion of the sea when with one full swoop the ocean inundated the proud cities of Cantre'r Gwaelod through Seithenyn's drunken aberration—cannot now be determined. But the most plausible, as well as the most reasonable conclusion that can be arrived at from a study of the conformation of the surrounding coasts is, that the ancient margin of the sea lay at the opening of the two estuaries—in a line with the Morfa Harlech and Morfa Bychan shores. The sea by gradually advancing, step by step, from century to century, at last over-ran the whole of the lowlands, since designated Traeth Mawr and Traeth Bach, and only found unsurmountable barriers to oppose its conquering march when it reached the mountains of Eryri. We find Sir John Wynne, of Gwydir, complaining in 1625, to his friend, Sir Hugh Myddleton, that "The fresh currents that run into the sea are both vehement and greate, and carie with them much sand; besides the southerly winde usually bloweth full to the haven mouth, carrieth with it so much sand, that it hath overwhelmed a greate quantitie of ground," &c., which shows that the sea continued to encroach at that period, and that its advance created uneasiness in the minds of the landed proprietors having estates bordering on it. The honour of giving birth to the idea of resisting these encroachments of the sea, and reclaiming the lands it had gradually absorbed is due to Sir john Wynne. It was probably suggested to his mind on his visits to a part of his property, which was in close proximity, and bordering on the sea, whose ravages was fully exposed to his view. But although, as he quaintly observes, "I ever had a desire to further my country in such actions as might be for their profit, and leave a remembrance of my endeavours." He felt himself unable to undertake a work of such vast extent, and confesses, "My skill is little, and my experience none at all in such matters . . . and have only wished well and done nothinge." He therefore opened his bosom to his more practical and experienced countryman and friend, Sir Hugh Myddleton, and forwarded to him the following letter:—

"RIGHT WORTHIE SIR, MY GOOD COUSIN, AND ONE OF THE GREAT HONORS OF THE NATION.

"I understand of a greate Work that you have performed in the "Isle of Wight, in gaininge two thousand acres from the sea, I "may saie to you what the Jewes said to Christ: 'We have heard "of thy greate workes done abroade, doe somewhat in thine own "countrey.'

"There are too washes in Merionethshire, whereon some parte "of my being lieth, called Traeth Mawr and Traeth Bychan, of a "greate extent of land, and entering into the sea by one issue, "which is not a mile broad at full sea, and verie shallow. The "fresh currents that run into the sea are both vehement and greate, "and carie with them much sand; besides the southerly winde "usually bloweth fulle to the haven's mouth, carrieth with it so "much sand, that it hath overwhelmed a great quantitie of the "ground adjacente. There is, and also in the bordering countreys, "abundance of wood, brush, and other materialls fit to make mounds, "to be had at a verie cheape rate, and easilie brought to the place, "which I hear they doe in Lincolnshire, to expell the sea. My skill "is little, and my experience none at all in such matters, yet, I ever " had a desire to further my countrey in such actions as might be "for their profit, and leave a remembrance of my endeavours; but "hindred with other matters, I have only wished well, and done "nothinge. Now being it please God to bring you into this countrey, I "am to desire you to take a ride, the place not being above a daies "journey from you; and if you do see the thing fit to be undertaken, "I am content to adventure a brace of hundred pounds to joyne you "in the worke.

"I have leade ore on my grounds in greate store, and other mine-"rals near my house; if it please you to come hither, being not above "too daies journey from you, you shall be most kindly wellcome,— "it may be you shall finde here that will tend to your commoditie "and mine. If I did knowe the day certaine when you would come "to view Traeth Mawr, my son, Owen Wynn, shall attend you there, "and conduct you thence to my house. Concluding me verie kindly "to you, doe rest,

"Your loving cousin and friend,

"J. WYNN."

" GWYDIR, 1ST SEPTEMBER, 1625.
"The honored SIR HUGH MYDDLETON, KNT., BART."

What if Sir John had been told that instead of a "brace of hundred pounds," it would require more than a hundred *thousand* pounds to expel the sea. His friend, Sir Hugh Myddleton, in the following letter, delicately hints that he was not

aware of the magnitude of the undertaking, and that to gain the
drowned lands it would require great sums of money to be
be spent, not hundreds, but thousands?   He excuseth himself
from embarking in this scheme of Sir]ohn Wynn's in this
wise:—

> "HONORABLE SIR,—
>
> "I have received your kind letter.   Few are the things done by
> "me, for which I give God the glory.   It may please you to under-
> "stand my first undertaking of publick works was amongst my owne,
> "within less than a myle where I hadd my first beinge 24 or 25
> "years since, in seekinge of coals for the town of Denbigh.
>
> "Touchinge the drowned lands near your lyvinge, there are
> "manye things considerable therein.   If to be gayned, which will
> "hardlie be performed without great stones, which was plentifull at
> "the Weight, as well as wood; and great sums of money to be
> "spent, not hundreds, but thousands; and first of all his Majesty's
> "interest must be got.   As for myself I am grown into years, and full of
> "busines here at the mynes, the river at London, and other places,
> "my weeklie charge being above £200, which maketh me verie un-
> "willinge to undertake anie other worke; and the least of theis,
> "wether the drowned lands or mynes, requireth a whole man, with
> "a large purse.   Noble Sir, my desire is great to see you, which
> "should draw me a farr longer waie; yet, such are my occasions at
> "tyme here, for the settlinge of this great worke, that I can hardlie
> "be spared one howre in a daie.   My wieff being also here, I can-
> "not leave her in a strange place.   Yet my love to publick works,
> "and desire to see you (if God permit) maie another tyme drawe me
> "into those parts.   So with my heartie commendations, I commit
> "you and all your good desires to God.
>
> "Your assured loving couzin to command,
>   "HUGH MYDDLETON."
> "LODGE, SEPT. 2ND, 1625.

This letter seems to close the correspondence, and the bold
project conceived by Sir John Wynne was doomed to remain
unaccomplished, for nigh two centuries.   But if Russia boasts
of her Peter, whose genius and perseverance reared the granite-
built capital his empire on the swamps and morass of the
emboguing of the Nera,—a capital which vies in splendour and
magnificence with the most renowned of European cities,—
Wales may also feel proud in the name of her Madocks, whose
enterprise and untiring energy grappled with, and broke through
accumulated difficulties and obstructions, and threw a barrier
against the aggression of the sea, thereby rescuing from its
grasp a tract of about 7000 acres extent of land, nearly all
available for cultivation,—and founding a place which will bear

his name down to remotest ages. And the merit of his actions do not diminish in lustre by this comparison—for had not one the population and sinews of an empire at the back of his arbitrary will,—while the other had to contend with monetary and other difficulties that would have crushed the energy of any other man? Mr. William Alexander Madocks, the great founder of this place, and the originator of most of the improvements in this part of the country was born on 17th June 1773. He was the third son of the eminent barrister of the same name, residing at Mount Masket, near London. After passing through the usual course of education, he was sent to complete his studies to the University of Oxford; where he highly distinguished himself as a scholar.

About the end of the last century, he came to reside at Denbighshire. Here he appears to have laid his hands on the above correspondence between Sir John Wynne and Sir Hugh Myddleton, and being in quest of an estate to invest the large sum of money bequeathed to him by his father, he came over to View the subject of the correspondence. Being of a highly speculative cast of mind, and seeing the capitalists there were for improvement and for farming a valuable district, he purchased an estate between Penmorfa and Traeth Mawr, in 1798, buying several farms from the trustees of the present Mr. Price, of Rhiwlas, Mr. Wynne, of Peniarth, and several small freeholders. The greater part of this property formed the valley now of Tremadoc, and was chiefly a wild unproductive marsh, most of which was overflowed by the sea every tide. Near to where a ditch that now flows out of the plantation, and under the high road near Tremadoc, was the bathing place of the folks from Penmorfa (the name of this village, the only one near there, signifying the "Head of the Marsh"). At this date, no formed road crossed this property—the high road, or horse road, from Lleyn towards England, passing through Penmorfa, and then over the rocks and hills out of the tide's way to Beddgelert, and for Merionethshire and South Wales across the sands and waters of "Traeth Mawr," which at nearly all times was dangerous, and frequently caused a loss of life. Mr. Madocks was not the man to remain idle after completing the purchase of his estate. He immediately commenced (22nd March, 1800) his great improvements,—one of the first being an embankment of earth carried right across the valley from Trwyn y towyn to Porth yr aiddyn, extending upwards of two miles, whereby he secured nearly 2000 acres of land from being overflowed by each incoming tide, and which now produces excellent crops of wheat, barley, clover, &c. After completing this (in Sept. 1800), he built the town called after himself— Tre Madoc, the site of which previous to that year being covered by 9 feet depth of water at the flow of the tide. "At that period there were within the protection of this embankment two cottages upon the islands, containing eight souls." (Original manuscript). He erected a house for himself— Tanyrallt—where he resided for many years, and exercised the greatest hospitality to a numerous circle of friends who were induced to come to Tremadoc by the wonders he wrought in the appearance of the neighbourhood. He also prevailed on some gentlemen to erect houses about—such as Ty Nanney, by Cae Nanney,—Morfa Lodge, by Mr. Robert Morris. To induce parties to settle in his new town, Mr. Madocks built at his own expense, a handsome Church in the late style of English architecture, which, while yet adding much to the beauty of the scenery, is a great accommodation to the surrounding English residents. He, also, generously built a Chapel for the accommodation and wants of the Welsh part of the population. Also, a Market house: the first market was held on the 8th day of November, 1805. Above this, a handsome Assembly-room was made, which was then occasionally used as a Theatre for private performance—several celebrated characters being brought down—Mrs. Billington for one. He established races at Morfa Bychan, to which race horses were sent from distant parts of Wales. But perhaps the most wonderful of Mr, Madocks' doings was the erection of a Factory, capable of containing 60 looms for broad cloths, where all the improved machineries in that branch of manufactory were used, together with a Dye-house and Fulling-mill. We have no means of learning the amount of business done at the Factory, but it must have been considerable while it lasted. By the end of 1809 there were 68 houses, and 303 inhabitants in and about Tremadoc.

Far from being satisfied with these splendid results, Mr. Madocks only saw in them the foreshadowing of still greater achievements. The striking success that had attended the construction of his first embankment, greatly enhanced the desire he had to put a complete check on the devastation of the sea, by rearing a bulwark boldly across the estuary, from Ynys towyn on the Carnarvonshire side, to Penrhyn isa' on the Merionethshire side. By carrying out this, he would not only Secure and reclaim some thousands of acres of land, but also form a good and safe communication between the two counties, and protect the Porthyraiddyn embankment from being breached and damaged by the floods and spring tides—which was most annoying and costly to repair. Towards effecting this object, he took the necessary measures for obtaining the consent of the owners of properties on the banks of Traeth Mawr, and then went to Parliament for powers to enable him to make such embankment, and for granting a certain portion of the reclaimed lands to himself and his heirs. Being in Parliament himself (for Boston, in Lincolnshire), and having considerable weight and interest in the House, he obtained a Bill in 1807, for accomplishing the above objects. The Bill was brought into Parliament by the late Lieutenant-General Sir Love Jones Parry, Madryn Park. Mr, Madocks immediately set to work, and having bought the Farm Penrhynisa' referred to above for the purpose of having a supply of stones to make the breakwater from the Merionethshire side,—commenced the work in March, 1808. From 300 to 400 men were constantly employed, blasting the rocks at the two ends, loading and unloading the Waggons, &c. This was a great boon to the surrounding country, food then being very high, employment scarce ere this undertaking was commenced. As the embankment drew near completion, and the pieces from each side advanced nearer one another, the difficulties and obstacles increased and grew more serious. The incoming and outgoing tides acted as saw on the two ends, and carried away in an hour what had cost several weeks labour to deposit. To overcome the difficulty of closing the gap, several vessels loaded with stones were sunk, and an immense quantity of piles fixed. Finally all obstructions were surmounted, and a line of communication was established between the two shires of Carnarvon and Merioneth, in 1811. To Mr. Madocks and his friends this event must have afforded the highest gratification. To see his exertions thus rewarded, and his enterprise thus crowned with success, was indeed an ample repayment for all his troubles and anxieties. But his mind was not doomed to remain long the abode of the sweet emotions produced by this great triumph. He was despoiled of his victory, and cast down by the cold breath of misfortune. On the 14th of February, 1812, the sea rose to a great height, the wind blowing in a hurricane from the West. After successfully encountering this storm for some time, the embankment at length gave way about the middle, and the sea rushing through the breach with immense impetus, for awhile carried everything with it, and made a very wide opening. Mr, Madocks was spared the pain of observing this disaster— being just then away from home. But having, as every great man has, an intuitive knowledge of the capabilities of his fellow-men, he had selected as the superintendent of his works a man uniting the most unswerving energy with a remarkable good sense and tact, and in every way worthy of the trust and confidence of such an employer. The late John Williams, Esq., of Tuhwnt i'r Bwlch—to whom we refer—was a native of Anglesey, and was born on the 9th day of May, 1778, at Ty'n Llan, in the parish of Llanfihangel Ysceifiog. Mr. Madocks and his undertakings attracting universal interest and attention throughout North Wales, he was induced early in life to leave his parental roof, and direct his steps towards the wonderful district of Traeth Mawr. Here he displayed such talents that Mr. Madocks was led to entrust to him the chief management of his numerous enterprises. This was a most fortunate choice for Mr. Madocks, and one that saved his darling projects from destruction and ruin. His faithfulness, perseverance, and ability, secured him not only the confidence and reliance of his employer, but also his friendship and love. To obey and effect the commands of such a man were labours of love, and far removed from a spirit of servility. Having watched Mr. Madocks' designs in their embryo state, and superintended them until their final accomplishment, Mr. Williams threw his whole heart into the undertaking, and exerted all his powers, when the Traeth Mawr Embankment was determined upon, and to the services he rendered may be chiefly ascribed the execution of that immense work. What pain, what anguish of mind must he have suffered then, when he saw what had cost him so much labour and anxiety made void by the angry waves of the sea! and this, too, when Mr. Madocks was some hundreds of miles away from the scene of the calamity. But his was a great soul—a soul that rose superior to difficulties—a soul that only saw in obstacles objects to be surmounted, and whom the storm shook but to infuse a greater strength into its roots.

Mr. Williams instead of succumbing to the disaster, with

alacrity determined to do everything possible towards repairing the injury. Immediately the occurrence happened, he forwarded circular letters, and messengers to every person whom he thought could render him some help—soliciting assistance in men, horses, &c. Never was a request made that received such a prompt and general compliance: gentlemen from Anglesey, Denbighshire, and Merionethshire at once sent him their contribution of men and horses, accompanied with letters expressing their condolence and grief at the untoward event that had occurred, while Carnarvonshire itself was in general commotion as if the scene of a revolution. The roads were crowded with men and horses, repairing with the greatest haste to the place of rendezvous. At every village groups were seen discussing the matter, and the subject of conversation in the palace and the cottage was the breach made by the sea in the embankment of Mr. Madocks, who was looked upon as a great benefactor by every class of people. When he heard of this general uprising in his favour, he was deeply moved and affected, and as he expressed himself to Mr. Williams: "The ready assistance given you by my neighbours I feel very sensibly . . and you will express to all my friendly neighbours how sincerely obliged I feel to them for their very handsome conduct. . . . To yourself, also, I wish to express my sentiment in very strong terms. Your manliness and resolution deserve every praise. No doubt, the experience last year in closing, and your own good sense and judgement make me feel more easy as to the steady and effectual restoration of the damage."

But this extraneous help was not enough to meet the emergency. Large sums of money were required for the purchase of timber, and other necessary articles, and to hire men and horses in addition to those sent by his friends, and also to pay for the food and shelter of the latter. It was with great difficulty that Mr. Maddocks, who had been obliged to borrow money to a large amount, was enabled to raise the necessary funds to meet the requirements. At this time he had let Tanyrallt to Percy Byshe Shelley (the poet), who was of very great assistance to him in obtaining aid to make good this damage, by making a crusade through the counties of Carnarvon and Anglesey, calling not only upon gentlemen individually, but also holding public meetings, to solicit aid, pointing out the great advantage to the country of the project Mr. Madocks had, in a great measure, successfully carried out.

The gap was gradually closed, and by the end of 1814, the repair drew near completion. But long before this Mr. Madocks had sketched out other schemes and improvements, as the following extract from a letter he wrote to Mr. Williams, dated Aberystwith, 9th December, 1814, shows: "I assure you I employ my mind incessantly in thinking how to compass those important objects necessary to complete the system of improvements in Snowdonia, any one of which wanting, the rest loose half their value. If I can only give them *birth, shape*, and *substance* before I die, they will work their own way with posterity. They would never enter into the head of posterity, or if they will, posterity might want the heart and hand to execute them,—have neither inclinations, or means, or if one, want the other. There is another important consideration too at the present moment,—the precarious state of the property; for if it does not advance, it will recede. It will not be stationery like the mountains around it. It will go backward if not forward, and the further it goes into decay, the more rapidly at last will it arrive at destruction. These are important considerations to add to the inducements to complete the system in all its parts, and to reckon nothing done, till the harbour and the railroad, which includes all additions and repairs necessary to the perfect security of the bank are established, and the road to Harlech, with the Traeth Bach Bridge opened,* a line to Trawsfynydd following of course. Nor until the clay-burning system is introduced generally—the very best means of improving the agriculture,—nor until means are taken to attract sea-bathers, for which the steam-boats from Liverpool have made so good an opening. None of these things will be done by posterity, and they are all so dependent on each other, that many of them, separately, would not have their due effect, unless the most part were done." In another letter he exclaims, "Thank God! the embankment is safe—that is the *keystone* to everything, to our success, our triumph, our security, our glory, and our emancipation from difficulties."

---

* Mr. Madocks had succeeded in getting a Bill passed, giving him power to erect a bridge over the Traeth Bach. He wrote to Mr. Williams on the 21st June, 1809 :-

"MY DEAR JOHN,—

The Act of Parliament for building a bridge over Traeth Bach received the Royal assent this day. I have had much trouble about it, and ten days ago thought I could not have carried it. However, Ministers have not been able to jokey me this time.—Yours, &c, " W. A. M."

As mentioned before, where Portmadoc now stands was up to this time a sandy waste, or a heap of sand-hills, any business that was carried on with shipping being done near to the Bar, at a place called Ynysgyngar. Being an exposed situation, vessels were in great danger of running ashore, and sustaining heavy damages, should a storm on a sudden occur. After the embankment was restored and completed, the water pent up in Traeth Mawr flowing out through the sluice gates at the Carnarvonshire end, gradually carried away the sand heaps, and by forming a deep channel along the side of the rocks, &c., showed that a harbour could be made at what is now called Portmadoc.

This Mr. Madocks saw, and consequently went to Parliament again for powers to form a harbour at Portmadoc, and to entitle him to dues. Though his bill met with a captions and impolitic, yet a powerful opposition, he ultimately succeeded in carrying it through Parliament, and it received the Royal Assent June 15th, 1821. The limits of the new harbour were thus defined and determined: "A line from the extreme point from the said embankment of certain lands called Trwyn y Penrhyn to the extreme point from the said embankment of certain lands called Garth Penyclogwyn, and from such line up to the said embankment—provided nevertheless that all ships and vessels loading or unloading cargo or cargoes, or any part or parts thereof, in the Traeth Mawr, between Garth Penyclogwyn and southern part of Garregwen, shall be deemed and taken to be within the limits of the said harbour." When the above act was passed, Portmadoc may be said to commence, as previous to this time (within a year or two) only three houses had been built on the sands, besides the house occupied by Mr. John Williams—Ynystowyn—which was a succession of additions that had been made to the blacksmiths, joiners, and other shops. At this time there was only one slate quarry in active operations in the neighbourhood of Festiniog, the one worked by Messrs. Turner & Cassons, shipping at that time slates to the tonnage of about 10,000 tons per annum. The late Lord Newborough had commenced one upon his property near Festiniog, but had not opened it to that extent to be a shipper of slates. There had also been a quarry opened on Crown property on Manod, but not being productive, was not then in work. A small work had been begun near Bwlch Carreg-y-fran, by Messrs. Roberts and Lloyd, but they had few or no slates to ship. In 1820, a Mr. Samuel Holland, from Liverpool, obtained a lease from Mr. W. G. Oakeley, to try for and work a slate quarry on his property at Rhiwbryfdir, and as this promised well in 1821, it gave a little stimulus to Portmadoc—Mr. Madocks incurring the required expenditure to confirm the Harbour Act to him by erecting a small quay, and doing some other works, which were done October 21, 1824. Vessels employed in carrying slates now came up regularly to Portmadoc, or near to it, to meet the boats which brought the slates down Traeth Bach from the quarries before alluded to, and a few more cottages were erected at the Port, which was still in a great measure a waste and overrun with gorse.

As the quantity of slates shipped increased yearly, and other businesses or trades sprung up, Portmadoc necessarily grew in extent and population with the improved state of trade. Mr. Madocks had for some years ceased to be a resident in the neighbourhood, having married, and gone to reside at the Hay, Breconshire, only occasionally coming down. When he did, he stopped at Morfa Lodge, and had the satisfaction to observe the improved state of affairs, and saw several good farms flourishing on the lands he had reclaimed,—Portmadoc rapidly rising into an important place, and his schemes developed and worked out in a satisfactory manner.

Amongst other projects started by Mr. Madocks was the endeavour to get Porthdynllaen adopted by Government in-stead of Holyhead, as the port of communication by packets with Ireland, and to form a new road from there (Porthdyn llaen) through Tremadoc, Beddgelert, &c., to Shrewsbury, and so on to London. Strenuous efforts were made by other parties to get Holyhead fixed upon, and a road made from there to Shrewsbury. A Committee of the House was appointed to hear evidence as to the relative merits of the two projects, and through the late Duke of York (in consequence of his quarrel with Colonel Wardle, who was Mr. Madocks' brother-in-law), did all he could in favour of the Holyhead party. Mr. Madocks' project was only lost by *one* vote. Had his scheme succeeded Porthdynllaen would have been the favoured port, the great travelling road between Dublin and London would have passed through Tremadoc, and most probably the Menai Bridge would never have been constructed.

Though baffled and defeated in many of his projects, and

the shafts of the envious were then directed towards him, he was never cast down, but drew consolation from the recesses of his own mind, and the good he had attempted to do. In a letter to Mr. Williams, speaking of some people possessed of an envious and malicious spirit towards him, he observes, "But I had rather have to reflect and look back on the good I have attempted to do, and hope I have done. Aye! and *look forward* too, to the good that will and must naturally flow in consequence of these actions, than have the *narrow minds*, and *bad hearts* of such contemptible and miserable human beings. The sun may yet shine, but when one feels to have acted from a desire to do good, *philosophy*, for which you say I have credit for possessing a great deal of, will come to our aid in a very consolatory manner in the most afflicting adversity."

In 1827, it became necessary for him to go to the Continent, and in 1829 he died in Paris, Where he was also buried. Thus closed the useful life of a man as distinguished for the benevolence of his heart, as for the vigour and brilliancy of his mind, and who, in seeking his own good, conferred inestimable benefit on this part of the country. His mind, though characterized by a remarkable breadth of conception, possessed an unusual power of grasping and shifting the details of every question brought before it for decision. His projects were therefore based on sound and endurable principles, such as could be carried out, and prove beneficial to posterity. His failing to develop some of these, and to compass and bring others to conclusion, was not owing to the weakness of his judgement, but to the exhaustion of his means. It is remarkable that every great improvement that has taken place in this district since the death of Mr, Madocks was first conceived and started by him. As early as 1814, it will be seen from the extract of a letter given above, his observation had been drawn to the desirability of connecting his proposed harbour with the quarries at Festiniog by a railroad. Besides the advantages that would flow to the slate companies from the establishment of such a certain and easy mode of transit, a railway, by bringing in the slates *direct* to Portmadoc, would be the means of imparting a stability to its trade, and conduce to draw other businesses to settle in it. Mr. Madocks had a line surveyed, We believe in 1824, but was not able to do more. In 1829, Mr. Holland, Junr., invited Mr. Henry Archer, the inventor of the stamps perforating machine, over to the neighbourhood, with a view to his forming a line, which he, after some preliminary steps, engaged to do, employing Mr. Spooner, now of Morfa Lodge, to make a survey of it in 1830. In 1831, he succeeded in getting a Bill introduced to Parliament to authorise the construction of such a line, &c.; but an opposition having been organised by the shopkeepers, publicans, carriers, boatmen, and other interested parties at Festiniog, Maentwrog, and on the banks of Traeth Bach, and a flaw being discovered in the proceedings for the Bill, it was thrown out. However, in the following year, 1832, he again went to Parliament, and though again opposed by the same parties, who fancied they should be injured by a railway being established, he succeeded in obtaining his Act, which received the Royal Assent the 23rd day of May, 1832. On the 26th day of February, 1833, the first stone of the railway was laid at Credd, by the late W. G. Oakeley, Esq., of Tanybwlch, and on the 20th day of April, 1836, the line was so far completed as to be ready for use,—a train of waggons laden with slates being brought down on that day from Mr. S. Holland, Junr.'s Quarries. Mr. Archer, or his Company (which he had then formed under the style of the Festiniog Railway Company) not having been able to arrange with the other parties working quarries at Rhiwbryfdir for the conveyance of their slates,—Mr. Holland continuing to be the only party using the railway until 1839, when the Welsh Slate Company took advantage of its facilities for conveying the produce of its quarry to Portmadoc.

The capital of the Railway Company was £25,000, and it borrowed £14,000 to complete the construction of the undertaking. Its dividend in many years has reached six, seven, and eight per cent. per annum. It conveys from 45,000 to 50,000 tons of slates annually to Portmadoc, and from there to the neighbourhood of the quarries about 2,000 tons of coal, lime, iron, flour, timber, &c.

The line Winds through beautiful valleys, thickly planted woods, and deep cuttings in the rocks, in its course from the quarries. Its length is nearly fourteen miles, forming an inclined plane the whole distance, the descent of which is about one inch in one hundred and twenty, the trains of loaded trucks consequently gliding down of themselves, and horses being required only to draw up the empty ones. Compared to other railways, the working expenses of this little tramroad are extremely low, and, therefore, its dividends very high. It has been of material benefit to the trade and business of Portmadoc by putting it in communication with the interior, and by affording an easy, cheap, and commodious means of transport to and from the populous district of the quarries, and thus centralising the commercial transactions of the district at this Port.

Immediately after the obtaining of the Railway Act, and it being known that the slates would be brought direct to it for shipment, the trustees of the Madocks estate caused wharfs and other conveniences to be made for their reception at an outlay of about £1,000. To these quays were afterwards added three others, erected by the Welsh Slate Company, Rhiwbryfdir Slate Company, and Mr. J. W. Greaves, and also a pier and break-water,—the cost of all these amounting to about £10,000. The Port itself rapidly increased in growth—houses and shops starting up, streets being marked out, and every encouragement being given to parties to build and settle in the place. One improvement succeeded another—business extended, vessels were built, and of larger and better class than formerly, the shipping trade made rapid advances, until the face of matters completely changed, and Portmadoc became a place of note, and commercial importance, realising in some degree the anticipations formed of it by Mr. Madocks. A In October 1838, his daughter, Miss Madocks (now Mrs. Roche) paid her first visit to the scene of her fathers extensive operations, and was received by the inhabitants with the most enthusiastic demonstration of pleasure, a public reception being given her. The address with which she and her mother were greeted was so appropriate that we cannot help transcribing it to our pages.

"MADAM,—It is with the liveliest satisfaction that we, the Com-
"mittee of the Tremadoc Hunt Ball, welcome you and your excel-
"lent mother to this scene of picturesque and romantic beauty, a
"spot which must awaken in your heart a thousand interesting emo-
"tions—a neighbourhood which owes a great portion of its charms,
"and all its adorning importance to the creative mind of one to whom
"you were from your birth an object of the tenderest affection,
"and the proudest hopes. Here you cannot look around you with-
"out beholding on every side memorials of his talents in devising
"the boldest and most gigantic plans, and of his energy and perse-
"verance in carrying them into execution. Here you may lau-
"dably cherish feelings of pride at the name you bear—a name
"which in this locality 'will never perish'—a name borne by that
"gifted individual before whom the proud waves retired, who clothed
"the barren sands with verdure, and made them smile with fertility,
"who on the desert erected habitations for the residence of men,
"and raised an alter for the living God. The Splendid effects of

"the skill and enterprise of that individual are not only obvious to
"the eye—they are experienced by all classes of the community.
"The extension of commerce, the outlay of capital, the increase of
"wealth discernible in this neighbourhood from year to year con-
"spire to attest the value of his services to the country at large,
"while they shew the just claims of his memory to gratitude and
"respect. We rejoice therefore in this opportunity of hailing the
"appearance of his daughter, his only child, among us, and more
"particularly on an occasion that is calculated to assist in rendering
"Tremadoc the centre of fashionable attraction, as it has already
become the focus of commercial activity. Permit us, Madam, in
"conclusion not only to flatter ourselves that this visit is the first
"step on your part towards a close connection, and a more frequent
"personal intercourse with this rising place, but also to express our
"sincere and ardent hope that wherever your lot may be cast, you
"may long live to adorn and bless the domestic and social circle,
"and to enjoy unalloyed happiness."

At the time of this visit, Portmadoc was only about the half
of its present size, and deficient of many of the conveniences
and institutions now in its possession. A post-office had been
established about two years before, say in 1836. In Mr.
Madocks' time the bags were carried by a man on horseback
between Carnarvon and Tanybwlch on alternate days—the
letters to Tremadoc being brought by a man on foot from
Beddgelert. Afterwards a post office was established at Tre-
rnadoc, and the mail conveyed by a car, and then by a daily
coach from Carnarvon via Beddgelert, Tremadoc, and Portmadoc, to Tanybwlch. Portmadoc had never enjoyed the
residence of a custom-house officer until about twenty-five
years ago. Previously, this official resided at Bryntirion, about
two miles distant from the Port, and though he had considerable duties to perform—there being duty levied on all coals
imported, and slates being subjected to a very heavy duty at
the port of discharge,—he still only occasionally visited the
Port. But in consequence of some representations made of the
inconvenience of this arrangement, the officer was directed to
reside in Portmadoc.

Coals, in consequence of the cruel impost saddled on them,
were very dear, and very seldom imported—only a cargo now
and then, and that divided amongst the inkeepers, and a few
resident gentlemen. However, in 1830, this harsh and injurous
tax was repealed, and instead of the 100 tons per annum before
imported, 2000 tons a year were discharged at this place in the
years following,—the poor participating with the rich in the
enjoyment received from this fuel.

The business transactions of the place increasing so rapidly, two banks were established—one a branch of the North & South Wales Bank, and the other of the National Provincial Bank of England. In 1847, a panic occurring amongst bankers, a run was made upon these, and the North & South Wales had to suspend payment, and though arrangements were eventually made for resuming business in some parts of the Principality, it was not done here. But the Messrs. Cassons, of Festiniog, opened a branch at this place, as well as at Festiniog and Pwllheli, and are, as well as the National Provincial Bank—which continues doing considerable business. A wish having been long and frequently expressed to have a Savings Bank established, where the labouring portion of the population could deposit their savings, a number of gentlemen enrolled themselves as trustees, and opened such institution in January, 1846. It has proved itself of great benefit to such as have availed themselves of its advantages, not only in times of sickness and want of employment, but also by instilling into them those habits of self dependence, industry, and economy that command happiness wherever they are found. Another establishment, to which we shall have to refer more particularly in another portion of the essay— the Mutual Ship Insurance Society—has wrought the most beneficial effects on the progress and prosperity of Portmadoc. This was formed in May, 1841, and under the auspices of Mr. Holland and Mr. J. W. Greaves, has gone on most satisfactory, enabling its members to insure their property at half the amount charged by other insurance offices.

As the population of Portmadoc increased, the want of a Market was very much felt, and it was resolved to make an effort to erect a Market Hall for the convenience of the public. By the vigorous action of a few gentlemen £600 was raised in shares of £2 10s. each, and a convenient Hall erected, in 1846, on a piece of land granted by David Williams, Esq., of Bron Eryri. County Court being required by Act of Parliament to be held in certain districts in each county, the large room that had been formed over the Market Hall was chosen as the County Court-room of this district. The rent received from this, from the store-houses, butchers stalls, &c., yield now an income which yearly pays the shareholders a dividend of 6 per cent.

Roads to and from Portmadoc have from time to time been greatly improved, and instead of there being only one leading through to Tremadoc and the summit of the embankment, there is now a very good one, made in 1836, alongside of, and below the top of the embankment direct to Tanybwlch, a less circuitous road to Criccieth, via Penamser, and another in course of formation that will afford a more direct communication with Beddgelert.

But perhaps there is nothing that more clearly demonstrates the immense progress that has taken place in this part of the country than the fact that land in the neighbourhood of Tre and Portmadoc purchased by Mr. Madocks at 2s. 6d. to 4s, an acre, is now let for 45s. per acre, and, naturally, for a higher rate than that when required tor building sites, &c.

The frequent wrecks, and cases of distress occurring in the Bay to large vessels inward bound to Liverpool, rendered it desirable that a Lifeboat Station should be established at some convenient point in the vicinity. The matter was taken up by N. Mathew, Esq., of Wern, and other gentlemen, and through their exertions a boat was secured from the Royal Mariners' and Fishermen's Benevolent Society,—the station being fixed at Criccieth, though chiefly supported by subscribers at Portmadoc. The services already rendered by it attests to its great worth and importance—not only as a means of saving life—but also of preserving property from destruction. On a late occasion, when the boat, on a dark night, steered for a vessel in danger of being wrecked on the causeway—it came across a French brig from Nantes, for Cardiff, which was within a few miles of the shore, carrying all her sails, with her head to the land, and had not the boat happened to meet her thus providentially, she would have been inevitably stranded and utterly lost.

In connection with this subject it may be allowed us to note the many efforts that have been made, from time to time, by the inhabitants of Portmadoc to induce the Government to erect a Lighthouse on Sarn Badrig (St. Patrick's Causeway). Though they do not, themselves, feel the least inconvenience or loss from this or other dangerous reefs in Cardigan Bay, all the replies received to petitions forwarded to Trinity Board amounted to the ridiculous announcement that they would be at liberty to erect one at their own cost if they wished, and this with the indubitable fact staring it in the face that from £5000 to £20,000 worth of shipping is lost *annually* from the nonexistence of this great desideratum! The vessels lost are mostly of Liverpool and American ownership, and therefore it is a much more serious matter for the consideration of Liverpool shipowners than those of Portmadoc, and other parts in Cardigan Bay.

The extension of the railway system to within twenty miles of this place, by the construction of the Chester and Holyhead, and the Bangor and Carnarvon Railways, has created a strong desire in the minds of the inhabitants of the surrounding district of participating in the accommodation, and the great benefits which flows from these iron thoroughfares, and this cannot be fully effected until a further extension into the neighbour hood is formed by a line from Carnarvon. Meetings have several times been held to agitate the subject, and surveys, sexions, and estimates have been made, but somehow things have been left in this state, and no company formed to compass the object. There exists no doubt but that a single line could be made at a cost of about £700 per mile, and such being the case it is a matter of regret that no decisive results have been arrived at. The traffic would be ample to secure a good dividend, as well as to cover the moderate expenditure that would be required, while the accommodation it would offer Carnarvonshire would be inestimable. We can only hope that when money becomes cheaper that some capitalists will be induced to undertake the formation of the line, and that landed proprietors will exhibit the same liberal spirit then as they have hitherto done. The carrying out of this project would afford great advantages to the slate trade of Portmadoc, of which it is now deficient, and place it on a par with that of Carnarvon, Port Dinorwic, and Port Penrhyn, by enabling the slate merchants here to forward slates direct to the inland districts of England by rail, and in other ways, which need not here be pointed out.

From 1841 to 1851, the trade and population of this place had been doubled. The latter year was made memorable to England by the Great Exhibition, and to Portmadoc by the National Eisteddfod held in it, on the 7th, 8th, and 9th day of October. But this congress of bards in Eifionydd had its precursors in an Eisteddfod held at Wern, Penmorfa, in 1793, when Gutyn Peris, Hywel Eryri, Richard Powell, &c., attended—the last named bard being the winner; and in the Eisteddfod held at Tremadoc, in 1811, under the patronage of Mr. Madocks, when Dewi Wyn won the prize offered for the best *awdl* on Agriculture,—Dafydd Ddu o Eryri being the adjudicator, and who, also, had prepared for the Occasion an excellent ode on the embankment, which was read at the meeting. But the Madog Eisteddfod of 1851, from the universal support rendered to it throughout the Principality, and from the extensive scale on which it was conducted, fully deserved to be called what it aspired to become, a National Congress of the Bards, Literati, and Elite of Wales. This resulted in a great degree from the diligence, care, and forethought shewn by the gentlemen form- ing the Committee, and in a pre-eminent manner from the labour and unwearied assiduity and devotion showed by their secretary, Mr. Thomas Jones, Cefnymeusydd, which terminated in one the most successful and triumphant meetings ever held in Wales. It was held in a Pavilion erected in the middle of the square, a spot washed by the sea before Mr. Madocks constructed the great embankment, under the presidency of the late Lieutenant-General Sir Love Parry. The prize for the Chair-poem on "peace " was awarded to the Rev. William Rees (*Gwilym Hiraethog*).

The prizes for the best compositions on the following subjects were awarded to the gentlemen whose names are placed oppo- site them, —viz :—

"An Awdl to the memory of Dewi Wyn."—Rev. T. Pierce, Liverpool.

"Cywydd to the memory of Robert Ap Gwilym Ddu."—Ioan Madawg.

" Poem on the Wisom of God."—Mr. Thomas Parry, Llanerch- ymedd.

"Poem on the Seaman."—Iorwerth Glan Aled.

"Elegy to the late W. A. Madocks, Esq."—Rev. W. Ambrose.

"Elegy to the late John Williams, Esq., Tuhwnti'rbwlch."— Rev. W. Ambrose.

"Poem on the fall of Jericho." (*Hirathoddeidiau*). Rev. W. Ambrose.

"*Englynion* on the Electric Telegraph."—Rev. W. Ambrose.

"Epitaph on Carnhuanawc."—Mr. Robert Hughes (*Robin Wyn*).

"Essay on the most effectual means of improving the minds and customs of the Welsh."—Mr. John Morgan, Wrexham.

"The working classes of Wales compared to those classes in England, Scotland, and Ireland."—Divided between Mr. Stephen, Merthyr, and the Rev. D. Griffith, Junr., of Bethel.

&c., &c., &c.

The proceedings of the Eisteddfod were conducted with great judgement and propriety—variety having been secured, which kept the interest in the entertainments from flagging. But how deplorable it is to think that an Eisteddfod which was brought to so happy a conclusion failed to yield the benefit which was

justly expected of it, the Committee of which falsified their pro-
mises of publishing the successful compositions, thus paralysing
the action of those means of intellectual advancement, and
moral elevation of the inhabitants of Wales.

After this great festival, no very important event has oc-
cured at Portmadoc. In 1853 an attempt was made by R.
A. Poole, Esq., to form a communication across the estuary of
Traeth Bach, but the estimate of the works shewing that the
erection of a bridge, and road in connection with it, would
cost £5176, and the annual revenue from tolls only calculated
at £274, the project was unwillingly abandoned, the sanction of
Parliament to it being deprived of.

By 1856, the Port had 200 houses, and a population of
about 1,300 souls. As we have avoided any particular description of it hitherto, we shall in the following chapter make
some observations on its sanitary state, its harbour, educational
establishments, and add some remarks on the moral, social,
and intellectual condition of its inhabitants.

CHAPTER II.

PORTMADOC AT THE PRESENT TIME.

HAVING presented to the reader some data bearing on the
history of Portmadoc, we shall now draw his attention to some
particulars connected with its present state. Situated by the
side of Moel y Gest—the scene displayed before this place is
magnificent, as well as picturesque. To the south the long
range of the mountains of Merionethshire appear—Harlech
Castle being a conspicuous object. This mountain rampart is
continued to the east—where Moelwyn and Cnicht rise their
heads proudly to the heavens, and then again to the north east
and, north—the wavy undulating form of y Foel Ddu and
Foel Hebog completing the chain of mountains almost encompassing this neighbourhood. The Glaslyn driven from its
natural bed by the construction of the embankment flows
through the sluice gates of a new Dock in course of formation,
round Ynystowyn, through Mr. Madocks' old sluice-gates, and
the present harbour, and empties itself into the sea. The town

is built in the form of a hollow square—one side wanting with terraces on its northern and western sides. London Road forms its eastern side, Osmond Terrace, &c., its northern,—Lombard street, Cornhill Street, and the Marine Terrace, its western side. Quays, carpenters' yards, &c., face it to the south. A small Park surrounded with a shrubbery occupies the hollow of the square. The houses,* about 200 in number, are all well and substantially built of stone,—and consist, generally, of a kitchen, parlour, and three bedrooms. Notwithstanding that there is too much of sameness in their construction, their appearance on the whole is neat and comfortable. The only drawbacks to be complained of are the underground cellars to be found in some parts, which are used as habitations, and the want of proper regulation for keeping the streets, &c., in order. No town can be more suitably situated for sanitary purposes than Portmadoc—merging on a rapid current flowing through its docks,—yet few places are to be found where the measures for the preservation of public health are more defective and neglected. Had it been more closely built—malaria, pestilential epidemics, and fevers would have found here a secure location— and had the cholera paid it a visit lately,—it is too dreadful to imagine where its ravages would have stopped. This state of things has arisen from divers sources—one being the limited space allowed by the Trust Estate as back ground to the houses—not sufficient in many instances to afford room for the erection of privies, ashpits, and other adjuncts necessary to the comfort of a family. Its neglecting on the other hand to introduce clauses into its leases to compel the lessees to open gutters &c., for carrying away the refuse water &c., and to provide for the proper drainage of the premises,—has been another powerful one. Had this been done from the first while it would have brought about a uniformity of sanitary arrangements that would have effectually prevented many of the evils existing at present,—damp unhealthy cellars, cesspools before doors, and the refuse matter thrown into the streets,— it would have entailed but a trifling cost on lesees. Another cause in conjunction with the last named one has been the grasping avaricious spirit of a section of the Leaseholders, which while forming these damp undrained cellars as habitations,

---

* The annual sum received as rents for the 200 houses amounts to £2000.

utterly neglected to provide privies &c., for the accommodation of the occupants,—thereby causing the nauseous sights too familiar to the eyes and olfactory nerves of the inhabitants and others. On summer mornings the effluvia emitted from the filthiness is most loathsome and disgusting. These remarks apply chiefly to the principal thorough-fare, London Road— and a part named Cornhill. The majority of the houses composing London Road have cellars underneath used as dwellings, which are almost invariably flooded in rainy weather. At the back of the street some small houses have been erected on the already limited space—these and the cellars are in most instances, deficient of the necessaries referred to above, and hence the dirt and want of decency. Cornhill exhibits the same traits—part of the refuse there being thrown into the dock,— and another, more economically, collected into an enclosure on the middle of the wharf for the purpose of being used as manure, and to emit its noxious exhalations for the benefit of the passers by. Although in winter the rain and cold weather mercifully act as sanitary agents and cleanse the streets of these pollutions, yet for the evils they displace—another discomfort then is suffered by the inhabitants—they have to wade in winter ankle-deep in mud and puddles along the streets, which are neither paved nor provided sewers to lead off the water. It seems to us that nothing can justify this indifference to order and cleanliness. As before remarked Portmadoc being in close proximity to the rapid current of the Glaslyn—no better or more advantageous outlet can be had for the discharge of its impurities. About 2 per cent. on the household property would amply cover the cost of opening main drains along the streets requiring them, and forming gutters branching from these for the drainage and cleansing of the cellars that are now so dangerous to the health, and baneful to the happiness of the residents. Other parts of the Port are free from these incumbrances, and beautifully clean, viz: Osmond and Marine Terraces, &c.

Another grievance under which Portmadoc labours is the absence of a bountiful, constant, and ready supply of water for domestic and other purposes. This is most severely felt from in the summer months, when the two springs and stream on which the inhabitants depend are partly exhausted and dried up. The servants sent to draw water are kept for hours waiting—sometimes through a great part of the night-thus causing a heavy pecuniary loss and inconvenience to families. Meetings have been frequently held with a view to remedy this matter, but although resolutions were framed and passed, no definite conclusion resulted from them. A copious supply of pure, sparkling, and delicious water might be easily obtained from a powerful spring at Beudy'rychain, a place about 1100 yards from the town, on the road leading to Criccieth. It is a pity steps have not been taken to turn this into use, which could have been done at a mere nominal sum. If pipes were laid down from the place to the Port, and four or more cisterns placed at each corner of the square, &c., as reservoirs, the defect would be both cheaply and effectually supplied.

During the winter of 1855, the streets were lighted with mineral gas, manufactured by Messrs. Holliday & Co., Huddersfield, the money for defraying the expenses being raised by public subscription. A Gas Company would undoubtedly reap good profits here. Many small towns of less size and wealth than this in Scotland, and England, and even in Wales are now lighted with coal gas. The subject has been often agitated, but hitherto brought to no tangible shape, which is much to be regretted, particularly when it is recollected how cheaply coal might be brought from Liverpool, and other places for the consumption. A company is now being organized for this purpose, and with the generous co-operation of Mr. D. Williams, of Bron Eryri, and other influential gentlemen, it is confidently expected to proceed.

Docks, Wharfs, &c. The dock accommodation hitherto available does not correspond with the wants of the commerce and trade of Portmadoc. The exports and imports having been doubled within the last 15 years—the present open dock—though about 5 acres in area, has been rendered insufficient,—vessels arriving and those ready to sail having usually to moor outside under the Rock Walk for want of space in the harbour. This is an exposed situation, and even dangerous during the prevalence of strong south and east winds. The want of a graving dock for the repair of vessels is much felt—the limited room allotted for this purpose causing much delay, loss, and confusion. But when the new dock in course of formation is completed, vessels then can be sufficiently accommodated and sheltered, as it covers nearly 20 acres of ground. The general depth of water is 18 feet at spring tide, and 8 feet at neap tides. Vessels have to pay harbour dues inwards if with a cargo (not otherwise) at the rate of 3½d. per ton, register tonnage, and outwards at the rate of 3½d, per ton*. The Wharfs have a frontage of about 700 feet five-sixths of which is devoted to the shipment of slates, the remaining one-sixth only reserved to the import trade, though this consists of 4000 tons of coal, &c., 4000 tons of limestone, and 5000 tons of general goods annually. The consequences are that the Harbour-master, though acting to the best arrangements, is obliged to subject ships to long detention before they are allowed to discharge their cargoes—particularly in winter, when the importation of goods is heaviest, and also to turn many off from the quay before they have had sufficient time to get rid of their goods. The existing provision for slate shipping also, though just enough for the present Slate Companies, can scarcely be called adequate should the Gorseddau, Isallt, and other quarry operations prove prosperous. But while pointing out these facts, we are glad to say that the new dock will furnish ample space for these various requirements of the Port.

A crane for discharging heavy and bulky goods is much required, and it must be conceded that the tradesmen, and others who receive such, have some claim to this as well as other conveniences being afforded them, when the following rates of dues levied on goods; in addition to what is imposed on vessels is considered, viz:—

Coal, Culm, and Coke .... 4d. per ton.
Iron, &c. .... 10d.   ,,
Powder.. 5s.   ,,
Timber.. 6d a load.
Flour, 2d., and Corn.. 1d. a sack.
Sugar, &c.. 3d. a cwt.
Furniture, Boxes, and Measurement Goods, ½d. a cubic foot, and other articles in proportion.

These rates are below those provided by the Act, 15th June, 1821,—the reduction having been affected through the influence and intervention of David Williams, Esq. The dues were recently let for a year for the sum of £1260, a fact that demonstrates clearly the large growth of the trade and commerce of a place only founded thirty years ago.

---

* This does not mean that a vessel is charged the *double* rate if she has a cargo *inwards and outward*:— in that case also she is only charged 3½ per ton register tonnage.

Its *places of worship* meet the wants of the population. Salem Independent Chapel was the first building erected for religious purposes. It was built in 1827, enlarged in 1841, and is again to undergo a further enlargement in 1856. The Calvinistic Methodists built a commodious chapel in 1845. The Wesleyans in 1840, the Baptists in 1841, between Portmadoc and Tremadoc, and the Scotch Baptists 1854. All of these are devoid of the least architectural pretension, and, with the exception of the Independents and Methodists Chapels, which are the best attended, are but small erections.

The *Literary and Educational Establishments* are less numerous than is desirable. A Reading Society, established in 1842, by the exertions of Samuel Holland, Esq., has, under his guidance, been carried on with great success. Though it languished for a year or two after its establishment, the Institution at last became to be appreciated, and as the room in which the members at first met did not afford the required accommodation, David Williams, Esq., built for them, at his own expense, a noble room (39 feet by 18 feet), and presented it to the Port for this object. Such an act cannot be too highly eulogised, and reflects the highest honour on its author. This room is justly adorned with a striking portrait of W. A. Madocks, Esq., having his finger placed on a paper purporting to be the charge of corruption against the Right Honourable Viscount Castlereagh and the Right Honourable Mr. Percival, dated May 12th, 1809.

The *Times, Globe, Shipping Gazette, Illustrated News, Punch, Liverpool Mercury, Marie Lane Express, Carnarvon Herald*, and *Amserau* newspapers are received into it. Also the *Quarterly Review, Dickens' Household Words, Chambers' Journal*, and the Welsh serials, *Traethodydd, Dysgedydd*, and *Drysorfa*. It is now very well attended, and has a library of about 250 volumes, many valuable works, having been lately munificently contributed to it by Mrs. Roche. This means of recreation and enlightenment provided at the annual subscription of 10s. cannot fail to leave the happiest effects on the minds and morals of the large number attending. The *British School* built in 1838, and situated equidistant from Portmadoc and Tremadoc, is generally attended by about 80 scholars. An old Seaman keeps a school at Portmadoc, and has about 40 children under him. These, with and addition of an establishment for young ladies.

form the educational means of this rising place—which has a population of 1300 souls, of which number, a third, at least, may be put down as children. This fact exhibits a lack of proper ideas of the value of education in the community—and, had this been our only criterion to form an opinion of the character of the population—unfavourable indeed must it have been. A National School is about being established—arrangements for the erection of buildings having nearly been settled. We trust that this is only a prelude to the shaking off of the apathy that has too long existed on this point, and that it will lead to the prosecution of further schemes for extending the blessings of education to every part of the community.

Population. Some few remarks on the present state of the moral, social, and intellectual development of the inhabitants will not be without their interest. Portmadoc being a comparatively new and advancing place, its population must necessarily present many of the phases peculiar to newly congregated communities, which are generally without the infinity, diversity, and distinctness of classes, so characteristic of the society of an old established town. The latter has, usually, on the one hand a select, exclusive, and carefully guarded circle of gentry, leading a life or luxury and pleasure while, it has on the other an opposite extreme,—a class of indigent poor, made up of those unfortunates created in society by time, and such of the labouring class as prefer idleness and starvation to labour and its accompanying comforts. But between these two strata, there is usually to be found an immense number of nicely defined layers, all having their various shades of respectability, and possessing different degrees of influence and importance, according to their status in society. The texture of the population of this place is very different,—it has not had sufficient time to settle into such nice distinctions and peculiarities. All of its classes being engaged in trade, and mixing in mutual intercourse,—the boundary lines separating them are not easily traceable nor definable, and hence they have an appearance of cohesiveness and uniformity not often observable in older communities. We should have had not the least cause to be sorry for this, had it not been in connection with another feature, partly arisen out of the same circumstances, and also from the inhabitants being an assemblage collected together from different parts by the trade and commerce of the place,—viz;

the want of proper and enlarged ideas of the value and importance of education.   Another deficiency worthy of being noted
is the want of an energetic public spirit in the community. To
this must be ascribed the unpaved, undrained, and, until very
recently, unlighted streets, and also the neglect shown of forming sanitary regulations for keeping the town in a decent and
decorous aspect, and for the defence of Public Health.   In these
respects, many a small place of not half the commercial importance of Portmadoc, throws it completely into the shade.

To particularize, we may be allowed to observe that the
gentry of Portmadoc and its neighbourhood are free from those
inflated ideas of themselves which characterise this class at
some other places, and act towards their less opulent neighbours as creatures possessing reason and intellect.   They are
also above those habits that make wealth a torment to its pos-
sessor, and a curse to a neighbourhood.   Their intellectual
activity is proved by the Circulating Book Society, carried on
by, and among themselves, which enables a member, by con-
tributing an annual subscription of a guinea to its funds, to
command the best works as they are published.   Among this
class, and meriting the highest esteem of the neighbourhood,
are those English gentlemen who left their country and migra-
ted into our bleak Wales, as it were in the hands of Divine
Providence, to bring out to the light of day the immense
treasures embedded in the mountains of Merionethshire and
Carnarvonshire, and who are distinguished for their liberality and
kindness to the numerous workmen employed by them, and
for their general cooperation in every scheme and measure
having the Welfare and the social and intellectual improvement of the inhabitants in view.

The establishment of the Portmadoc Ship Insurance Society, and its subsequent success, of the Savings Bank, and of
a Lifeboat Station in connection with the Royal Shipwrecked
Mariners and Fishermen's Society, at Criccieth, were all chiefly
accomplished through and with the aid of these gentlemen.

As to the tradesmen of the Port, it may be remarked that
they are, as a whole, honest, industrious, and economical; the
paucity of insolvencies and bankruptcies among them attests
to the first, while the fact that the greatest part of the house
and shipping property of the place is theirs, is an adequate
evidence of their diligent and economical habits.   They also
give the lie to that stereotyped, though utterly unfounded

remark, that the Welsh are deficient of the spirit of enterprise. Persons who give currency to this erroneous observation cannot have sufficiently considered the condition and circumstances of the people and their country, otherwise they could not have failed to arrive at another, and a more reasonable conclusion. This spirit requires incitements to call it into activity, is dependent on the state of a country, and must be nurtured and developed by time before attaining its full growth. English enterprise did not attain its present strength and development in one day, in one year, nor in one century. In its youth it required the help and guiding hand of the Lombard and Jewish Merchants, and has had six or eight centuries to arrive at its proud station in the present age. How then can it be expected that a comparatively poor and primitive nation that has been living in the seclusion of her mountain solitudes, and separated from the world around, as the Welsh nation has been, until lately, before the tread of the locomotive's iron hoofs disturbed the profound calm of her hills and vales,—should at once exhibit a trait created by a long course of successful commercial enterprises. So far as our observation extends, the Welsh have not budged an inch to their Saxon neighbours wherever they have come into contact with each other—when, enjoying similar advantages, and surrounded by the same influences. On the contrary, we have numerous evidences, even in Carnarvonshire, that they can enter into trading speculations with an energy and spirit worthy of the emulation of nations much more advantageously placed. Portmadoc, although a child as it were of yesterday, is able to boast that some of its vessels plough the Mediterranean, navigate the Black Sea, traverse the Atlantic, double the Cape of Good Hope, encounter the stormy billows of the Indian Ocean, or pass that dread of mariners—Cape Horn, and enter the placid waters of the Pacific Ocean, while the names of the different ports in the Baltic, and on the Western coast of Europe sound as familiar in the ears of the inhabitants as those on either side of the Bristol Channel, from the frequency of the visits which their stout and handsome little vessels have paid to them.

This reminds us of another class forming a large portion of the population, and deserving our warmest commendation,—viz.: Master Mariners. Whatever may have been the share British seamen had in placing England in her present commanding position amongst, the nations of the world, we can fearlessly assert of the Master Mariners of Portmadoc, that by their vigour, diligence, and upright conduct in their vocation, they have pre-eminently assisted in producing and establishing its present welfare, and have also laid down broad, stable, and sound foundations for its future prosperity and success. Wherever they have been with their slate cargoes, their conduct was such as to be an honour to their place of abode;—their sobriety and uprightness securing from those they came in contact with a favourable opinion of their moral character. All of them invariably have an interest in the vessels under their command, and by economy and assiduity, many of them have secured to themselves a respectable amount of property.

The labouring classes, comprising ship carpenters, mariners, smiths, labourers, &c., are both thrifty and frugal. While the trade and traffic of the Port supply them with abundance of work, their own general sobriety and frugality in the management of their earnings, give them an air of comfort and decency not always observable, even where plenty is bestowed. In these traits, the working men of this place present a remarkable and desirable contrast to those of many a small seaport that we could name. Here there are no drunken brawls and riots creating disquietude and disorder;—no Saturday night saturnalia desecrating the Sabbath, and continuing its orgies until the means of debauchery are finally exhausted,—and no scenes of misery and suffering that, without exception, accompany a course of habitual intemperance. The leisure hours are here generally spent in the bosom of the family, and consecrated to the duties arising therefrom. Will it be believed that, though its population amounts to 1300 persons, and frequented by about 2000 seamen every year, Portmadoc and its neighbourhood has not one police constable! Yet nowhere do peace and propriety hold a more thorough sway, and nowhere are the labours of that functionary less required. This single fact speaks volumes as to the moral state of the inhabitants. But it may be asked, what has given it this quiet and orderly aspect? We can be at no loss to reply. It must have been produced from the prevalence in the community of the principles of revealed religion, and is not the transitory result of any artificial system. Whatever may he its deficiencies in an educational point of view, there is not (comparatively speaking) any cause to complain of indifference to the means and ordinances of religion.

Although Portmadoc cannot claim to be the birthplace of

an illustrious person, it is well-known as being the abode of two eminent contemporary poets, who have conferred a lustre on its name which centuries cannot efface. We allude to the Rev. William Ambrose (*Emrys*), and Mr. John Williams (*Ioan Madawg*). Mr. Ambrose was born at Bangor, on the 1st day of August, 1813. His ministerial connection with this place has been of eighteen years duration, and of the greatest influence and importance in forming the moral and social character of its society. It will not be expected of us to enlarge on the characteristics of his oratory and poetry. His ministerial orations are free from the flatulent allusions and uncouth jargon too generally indulged in, and are distinguished for their chaste simplicity, clothing the noblest philosophical thoughts in such a simple garb that the weakest intellect in his congregation can comprehend depths which less skilful orators would have converted into "confusion worse confounded." His *Awdl* (Ode) on the "Creation" is characterised with great purity of conception, striking illustrative beauty of language, and a classic symmetry of parts. Though deemed unworthy to rank as the first of the poems sent in to the Aberffraw Eisteddfod, in 1849, by two of the adjudicators, the public and literati of Wales, have generally endorsed the fiat given by Eben Fardd on the merit of the composition, and given it the first place. The imagery of the elegy on the late Mr. Madocks is only equalled by the plaintive diction in which the bard expresses his sorrow, while the poetical feeling combined with the true pathos displayed in another elegy on the late Mr. Williams, of Tuhwnti'rbwlch— have produced a piece of poetry the equal of which we have but rarely seen. These two pieces, together with some vigourous *englyion* on the "Electric Telegraph," and a piece on the "Fall of the Walls of Jericho," were the successful compositions on the subjects, at the Madoc Eisteddfod, in 1851. His poem in memory of four of the noblest sons of Wales, viz.: the Rev. Evan Jones (*Ieuan Gwynedd*), Morgan Howells, John Jones (*Tegid*), and Dafydd Rhys Stephen, which gained for its author the prize of twenty guineas offered by the Aberystwith Literary Society, 1853, favourably exhibits the universality of his poetical traits and genius, and when published was hailed with the general acclamation of his countrymen. But the star of his poesy had not then reached her culminating point. The 25th of July, 1855, witnessed our author the triumphant Chair Bard of the Royal London Eisteddfod—the subject of the *awdl* being "Patriotism" (*Gwladgarwch*). The adjudicators remark respecting it: "It abounds in sweet and vivid illustrations of the subject, delicate touches, and noble aspirations; though some few *cynghaneddion* may perhaps be thought wanting in strength and precision, its rich poetry, fine taste, and classic elegance, more than compensate for the few minor blemishes it may contain. To "Bleddyn," the gifted author of this brilliant poem, we therefore award the prize." He is the author of many minor poems of very great merit:—*Awdl* in memory of Ioan Powys, *Cywydd i'r Haul*, &c., &c.

Ioan Madawg is the Burhit of Wales, and many and bright are the sparks from his anvil. His father, Richard Williams, like himself a blacksmith, had a correct taste for poetry, and the son early felt its glow warming his bosom. He was born on the 3rd of May, 1812, at Cefnbychan, in the parish of Ruabon. His father removed from there to the neighbourhood of Portmadoc about the year 1819. His life has been one of unwavering industry—bodily and mentally. While holding a communion with the muses, his arm wielded the hammer, and while complying with their behests, he swerved not from the duties and realities of life. He has produced some pieces that rival anything published in the Welsh language. In his ode on the storm—the tempest verily seemed to rave in the wild nervous strength of the alliteration; in reading it we fancy we hear the craggy sides of mountains yawning, dashing, and crashing in wild uproar,—the strange moaning of the wind careering on its destructive course, laying low the firm-rooted oak, lashing the sea into fury, and taking the noble vessel in its arms, and dashing her against the rocks; we breathlessly witness the efforts of the crew to escape their watery grave,—but Oh!—

> "Dacw hwy'n safnau'r tonau tynion,
> Oll yn ymdrochi mewn llawn ymdrechion,
> Weithiau ar frigau ruthr-for eigion,
> A'i frig rhwygedig hyd fro Caergwdion,
> Wed'yn dan bwys dwys y don—llwyr soddi,
> I dyn galedi, yn y gwaelodion."

It abounds with passages that evince a descriptive power of the highest order. His *cywydd* on "The defence of Gibraltar, by General Elliot," victorious at the Aberffraw Eisteddfod, in 1849, contains some vigorous writing—the ring, roar, and strife of war are echoed and nobly portrayed in its fiery lines.

He was again successful at Rhuddlan, 1850, where he won the prize for a *cywydd* on Doctor Morgan. This one exhibits another feature of his poesy—a quiet beauty in the treatment of the subject that harmonises well with some minds. One of his happiest pieces is the *cywydd* in memory of the late poet, Robert ap Gwilym Ddu, which gained him the prize at the Madoc Eisteddfod—in which nature in her most lovely aspects is delineated, and her most bewitching beauties are brought in as similies. The quiet life of his brother bard—his feelings, flight of thought, and the scriptural tendency of his medita-tions and works are appropriately and pathetically described. But his unpublished *awdl* on the "Sufferings of Christ" we are disposed to place higher than either of the above. The grandeur of the imaginations, grouping of the incidents, and the vigour of the description, stamp it as a masterpiece, and its author as a true poet. He is the author of many small poems, which our space will not allow us to name.

Mr. Richard Williams (*Bueno*), a brother of Ioan, is also deservedly known to fame, and Mr. John Philips (*Tegidon*), has published some very excellent poems—displaying a correct taste, and a happy expression of ideas,—both of whom are residents of Portmadoc.

CHAPTER III.

THE RESOURCES OF PORTMADOC.

THESE are various, but may be classed under the heads of export trade, import trade, ship-building trade and shipping property. We shall first glance at its

EXPORT TRADE.

Slates form the bulk of it. But before detailing the rise and progress of the traffic in slates, it maybe desirable to offer some observations regarding the other mineral resources of the territory to which Portmadoc is the outlet. If these are unim-portant at the present time, it is from their not having been opened and explored to the extent which their known merit warrants. There can be no doubt that when this rich mineral district is connected with other parts of the country by railways, and the stream of mining enterprise directed towards it, these sources of wealth will prove of vast importance to the neighbourhood.   Hitherto slates have almost monopolised the attention of gentlemen interested in mining explorations in this part of the country, and thus indications of other minerals have not been attended to, and followed up as they deserved to be. *Copper* is found at numerous places about Beddgelert, and at Pantywrach, in the parish of Llanfrothen.   From 200 to 300 tons of it is annually shipped from this Port.   *Lead ore* of a very superior description is raised at Bwlchyplwrn Mine, the property of W.O. Gore, Esq.,M.P., and about a mile distant from Pantywrach in a north-eastern direction.   This mine was worked 500 years ago.   A tradition current in its vicinity says that it was first opened by the Romans in their excursions through Wales—one part of it being called by the miners, *Gwaith Romans*, or the Romans' Work.   Recently an old hearth for smelting the ore, and a lump of prepared lead of 15 lbs. weight were discovered.   These, as well as the small levels that are found in it, which are the size of the veins, and follow their course, point to a very remote period, and when powder was not applied to mining operations.   It has been worked by the two Mr. Hollands, of Plasynpenrhyn, since 1837, and at one time since then produced about 100 tons a year.   From one cavity alone 150 tons were extracted.   It has six seams which dip at an angle of about 45 degrees.   Contiguous to it is the Penyrallt Lead Mine, on the property of the Misses Richards, of Llanfairisa'—which was opened about the year 1825. From the one seam that has been worked, many hundreds of tons have been raised.   It was stopped some years ago, but again started towards the end of 1855, by a company who carry it on under the appelation of]ane and Catherine Consols' Mine.   The whole exports of lead do not amount to above 50 tons annually of late years.   Large deposits of *Iron ore* exist at Llidiart Yspytty and Pensyflog, both within a mile of Portmadoc.   In 1848, 1849, and 1850, from 10,000 to 15,000 tons of ore was raised at these places, and forwarded to South Wales, but the works have since then remained at rest. *Sulphur* has been raised in 1854 on the lands of Hendre ddu and Ymwlch bach farms, near Tremadoc, and also large quantities have been raised at one time from the vicinity of Beddgelert.   Owing to the low price obtainable for the article, the works at these places have been abandoned. But to return to an article of far greater importance to Portmadoc than either of these, we shall devote some pages to record the history of the Portmadoc

SLATE TRADE.

The slate trade, from the preponderance of its importance, and its influence on the prosperity of the place, must be placed at the head of the resources of Portmadoc. We cannot fix the precise date when slates began to be exported from this neighbourhood. Probably the first slates shipped were from a small quarry at Bronyfoel, a farm situated on the western side of Moel y Gest. They were brought from the quarry to Ynysgyngar, in wicker hampers, on men's backs. The Festiniog quarries were gradually opened, and their produce also brought down Traeth bach, and shipped at Ynysgyngar. The prescient mind of Mr. Madocks, early conceived the immense benefit that would accrue to his newly founded harbour from linking those quarries with it by a line of railway. He, therefore, as an inducement to prosecute, and to facilitate the accomplishment of such a scheme, introduced a clause into the Act, June 15th, 1821, which provided that should a railway be made from these quarries to meet the Merionethshire end of the embankment, slates passing over it were not to he subjected to tolls, &c. He had a line surveyed in 1824. Having already related how this communication was formed and perfected, and its effects on Portmadoc, we next offer a sketch of the rise and progress of the Festiniog Slate Quarries. They are situated on the sides of a hollow between the Manod and Moelwyn mountains. The first explorations for slates were made on the eastern or Manod side of the hollow. Diphwys, the quarry first opened there, was begun about 1765, by Methusalem Jones and William Morris, two quarrymen from the Cilgwyn Quarry, Carnarvonshire. In 1769, several other quarrymen joined them, from the same quarter. These men worked the quarry under an annual rent, until 1800, when it was advertised for sale. Perhaps it is not generally known, that the Irish Rebellion of 1798, had a connection with the slate quarries of Festiniog. But so it was. A Cumberland quarrymen, named William Turner, worked at a small quarry of Admiral Mills', in Ireland. When the rebellion broke out, he and other English-

men growing solicitous about the safety of their lives, made
their anxiety known to their employer, the Admiral, who
promptly determined to leave Green Erin, to the tender care of
her Whiteboys, Ribbonmen, &c.   He came over to Conway,
where he was for some time engaged at a small quarry, employing Turner as his agent.   But Turner hearing that Diphwys
Quarry was on sale, or to be let, at once determined to travel
over the country to inspect it, and so pleased was he with the
survey that he instantly sent to two of his old friends in Cumberland, Thomas and William Casson, to come over and view
the work.   Without more ado, they complied, and fully con-
firmed the favourable opinion formed of it by Turner.   These
three resolute men set to work—secured a lease from Mr.
Wynne, of Peniarth, the father of the present Honourable
member for Merionethshire, W. E. Wynne, Esq., and with
some extraneous help, finally surmounted all difficulties—their
resolution and perseverance being soon rewarded with success,
and themselves with affluence.   All the slates that have been
made at this quarry have been brought to Portmadoc by boats.
It has been in operation for 55 years, and although partially, is
not yet fully exhausted, yielding now about 2000 tons of
slates annually.

Touching this quarry is *Cloddfa Lord*, so named from the
owners of the property—the Lords Newborough.   This was
partly worked by the late Lord Newborough, the father of the
present Lord Newborough, in 1801, but it was soon after stopped,
and remained in this quiescent state until 1823, when Lord
Newborough, brother to the present Lord, resumed the workings commenced by his father.   After expending about £15,000
during the year or two he worked the quarry, he eventually
leased it, in 1828, to the Messrs. Roberts, of Carnarvon, who
pushed it on more vigorously.   After holding it for 5 years,
and spending £30,000, they failed in 1833, and the quarry
reverting to Lord Newborough, it was let on lease, in the
beginning of 1834, to Messrs. Shelton & Greaves.   In this instance, it might well be said of these parties, "other men
laboured, and ye are entered into their labours."   After
£50,000 had been sunk by former proprietors, no sooner had
this party commenced working, than their enterprise was
crowned with success, and large profits reaped.   The quarry
was exhausted a few years ago, and another little work has

been recently opened by its side—the Votty Quarry, which has manufactured a few good slates.

The first trial for slates on the northern or Rhiwbryfdir side of the hollow, was made in 1814, by a Mr. Williams, of Machynlleth, Richard Griffith, and R. W. Solomon, on Talywaenydd farm, which was utterly condemned. In 1816, another search was made by a Richard Thomas, of Penmachno, which was also doomed to end in disappointment. In 1819, Samuel Holland, Esq., a gentleman well-known from his numerous mining enterprises in North Wales, negotiated and secured a lease of the Rhiwbryfdir farm, from the late William Griffith Oakeley, Esq., of Tanybwlch, for the yearly rent of £150, and a royalty of one-tenth of the value of all slates raised and manufactured. The previous rent of the farm was only £95, and Mr. Oakeley thought much more of the £55 advance in the rent of the land, than the sum he might pocket from the royalty on slates,—but what amounted to between £6000 and £7000 annually, at the present time. In 1825, there was a mania for working slate quarries in Wales and many companies for that purpose were formed in London. One of them, styled the Welsh Slate Company, of which Lord Palmerston and Lord William Powlett are partners, purchased from Mr. Holland a portion of this ground on which were the quarries he had opened, and pursued the workings there with great vigour. This company now constantly employs 450 men—yearly raising 19,000 tons of slates.

In 1828, Samuel Holland, Esq., son of the former Mr. Holland, who commenced the quarries, at Rhiwbryfdir, opened a new quarry on a portion of the Rhiwbryfdir farm that was not sold to the Welsh Slate Company, obtaining a fresh lease from Mr. Oakeley. This work now yields about 10,000 tons annually, and employs above 300 men.

In 1838 a company styled the Rhiwbryfdir Slate Company leased and worked one of Mr. Holland, Senior's trials, situated between the other two. Great success has been met with, as the 15,000 tons yearly made by them amply proves. About 350 men are employed.

With the exception of a narrow division between Mr. Holland's quarry and that of the Rhiwbryfdir Company, these three principal works, at the present time, form one great cavity. The scene here exhibited is so interesting and novel that we are tempted to describe it. Along the divisions, or galleries, into which the hollow is divided, are seen trains of waggons moving backwards and forwards. On the sides are seen men suspended by frail ropes over awful precipices, busy boring holes for blasting. Other men are engaged loading rubbish and slate slabs into the trucks, which are lifted up from the lower parts by means of water balances, and are then drawn by horses through dark levels, emerging at length at the rubbish heaps. But what means the sound of that horn? At once there is a general escape, as if from the scene of some dire disaster. Then follow the blasts—pop—pop—pop, until the very ground rocks—the surrounding mountains long reverberating the reports. Immense masses of rock are loosened—the slate rock rather gently, but the granite and bastard rocks with greater force. The bugle is again sounded, the men reappear from behind projections, strange holes, and clefts, and with alacrity resume their work. The clinking of hammers is once more heard throughout the extent of the great cavity.

John W. Greaves, Esq., opened a quarry in 1846, on the western side of a spur, intervening between the Rhiwbryfdir Quarries and the Diphwys and Lord Quarries. This work now produces about 4,000 tons of slates a year, and employs 150 men.

All the Works are on the same vein, which in one continuous line follows the configuration of the ground, from Diphwys and Lord to Llechwedd (Mr. Greaves), then to the Welsh Slate Company's, Rhiwbryfdir Company's, and Mr. Holland's Quarry. It is found again on the other side of the mountain, at the Cwmorthin Quarry, a small trial worked by W. B. Chorley, Esq., of London. Opposite to the last quarry, is the Wrysgan Quarry, now stopped for want of capital. The Rhosydd Quarry lies on the top of the mountain, near to these last workings. There are about 150 men employed, and a few slates have been made. There are several small trials in the neighbourhood, but scarcely deserving of any special notice.

Thus within the limit of half a century have these works sprung up, which now in the aggregate give employment *directly* to 1,500 men, to whom about £70,000 is yearly paid in wages,—and *indirectly* to many more. They manufacture 50,000 tons of slates every year, the estimated value of which is about £120,000. Here is observed the mighty change wrought by the commercial spirit of English enterprise, which has thus transformed bleak mountain wastes into sources of industrious occupation, private wealth, and national prosperity. To say that the agricultural and other interests of the neighbourhood have immensely profited from the quarries will be considered unnecessary. The development of one branch of industry always tends to the prosperity of other branches.

We shall not attempt to discuss the theories advanced by Geologists to explain the formation of clay slates. Whether it has been composed of the minute fragments of rocks carried away by the currents of rivers into some grand reservoir, and there subsiding into a sedimentary formation—layer on layer—the internal heat of the earth transforming it into thick clay, and gradually baking it into a slate rock, which through the action of a subterranean eruption, at a remote period, was elevated on the back of a protruding mountain, where man might be able to use it for his benefit and comfort—or whether by some secret process, known only in the laboratory of nature. What we have to deal with are the facts,—we leave it to others, more able than ourselves, to speculate, and draw conclusions from these facts. The direction of the slate stratum at the Festiniog Quarries lies east and west, with a dip to the north, at an angle of about 25°. The direction of the cleavage is at an angle of 45°. The slate bed lies between strata of granite of great thickness, layers of mixed bastard rock intervening. Occasionally, quartz is found between the bastard and slate rocks, and almost invariably a seam of it from 2 to 3 feet thick divides the latter into two portions—the quality of the material differing considerably in those two divisions. The seam follows the cleavage, and not the stratification of the rock. If situated on hilly ground, the slate stratum is generally found only covered by a moderate depth of earth and loose matter, but if in a hollow, the superincumbent waste is of great thickness. The excavations at these quarries show that the vein contracts as it deepens, indeed at the Lord Quarry, now exhausted, it was found completely enclosed between the granite rock. Though some portions are more easily worked than others, it varies but little throughout its extent.

The old mode of extracting the slate, and manufacturing it into roofing slates, was clumsy, tedious, and very damaging. Besides being unscientific, the early quarrymen were not provided with proper instruments and tools. Having cleared the rubbish off a piece of rock, they endeavoured with the wedge, hammer, and crowbar, to detach a piece, which having effected through great labour, they placed the block over a round stone, and then struck exactly over it with a large hammer, to shape it to proper dimensions. Thus they must have caused a great loss by committing a large amount of breakage. The pieces or blocks having been roughly shaped, were carried by men on their shoulders to the rubbish heaps, there to be made into different sizes of slates. After being split, the slates were cut or dressed wholly by conjecture, and often varied an inch or more in length and breadth, the measuring stick not being used then. Experience gradually discovered and supplied these deficiencies.

The first operation in quarry working as at present conducted is to divide the slate rock into divisions or galleries, the most convenient depth for working these quarries is found to be 15 yards.

Roads to draw away the water, and for the regular working of the divisions are the next necessaries to be provided. A road to some of the depths is easily formed, while to others, the encompassing hard rock must be rounded, or tunnelled through, to reach the slate rock. When roads are completed, the galleries are begun—the highest first, and then the others, each in advance of the next, lower down on the stratum. These are subdivided into *bargains*, or takings, and let to parties, who most commonly, consist of four men, two of whom are employed in boring, blasting, and roughly shaping the blocks into convenient dimensions to be sent away to the two others outside on the heaps splitting and dressing the slates. A bargain is begun either by making an opening under the hard rock, or by cutting through it from the surface, until the slate rock is reached. It will be evident to the reader that pillars of slate rock must be left at different intervals to support the overhanging mass if the first method is adopted. The rubbish and other waste are removed outside in iron waggons placed on tramroads, and the slate blocks on small trucks. All are weighed on machines placed at each of the tramroads, the labour of the loaders, horses, and unloaders being paid for at the rate of so much per ton. The blocks, some of them 7 yards long, having been deposited on the heaps, are then cut into proper lengths. This is effected by making a notch on one of the edges, and then giving a bold stroke exactly over it on the other edge, with a large wooden hammer, facetiously called by the quarrymen "Rhys". The piece will thus be cut straight across the grain of the material. It is afterwards split to the required thickness, with long iron wedges. The pliability of the material is such when just extracted that it will bend considerably, and may be split to the 1/32 part of an inch. Dry and frosty weather is not so favourable for splitting and shaping as wet weather. To observe the dexterous manner in which these operations are performed cannot fail to strike a spectator with amazement, and those men only who have been trained to this work from their boyhood acquire the skill and proficiency required.

Mr. Matthews, Mr. Greaves, and Mr. Holland, have each invented machines for dressing slates, which work well and correctly. The appearance of the slates cut by them is very beautiful. They are very applicable for cutting fancy slates: round, diamond, hexagon or gothic shapes, but it remains a matter of doubt whether any pecuniary advantage is derived from their adoption for general purposes. If the material be a little crooked, it is apt to break in being cut by them. The names of Princesses, Duchesses, Countesses, Marchionesses, and Ladies, given to several sizes by General Warburton, are now almost discarded at these quarries, the dimensions in inches being substituted, as 24 by 14 for Princesses, &c., &c. Several useful contrivances have greatly facilitated the working, and augmented the productiveness of these undertakings. The water balance has rendered the raising of rubbish, &c., from the lower depths a comparatively easy matter. These are employed at all the quarries requiring such work. The Rhiwbryf-dir Company have also a steam engine for this purpose, and to drive Mr. Mathews' slate cutting machines. Cranes and Grab Winches are now generally used to raise large pieces of granite on the trucks,—formerly much labour and expenditure were consumed in blasting these, in order to effect their removal. A large plant, it will be readily conceived is required for opening and working a quarry. Iron rails, waggons, water balances, cranes, chains, ropes, and timber, make up the greatest part of it. To this must be added the great consumption of powder, candles, oil, &c. Inclined planes and their machinery, help to swell up the cost at these quarries. But this is less expensive than the steam engines required for such as may be placed in low situations. After the slates are loaded into trucks, these latter are let down by means of inclines, to the line of the Festiniog Railway, and conveyed to Portmadoc as before related. There, vessels having been placed along the sides of the quays, the slates are slid down on planks, and handed into the hold, where they are stowed closely and with the greatest care. So efficiently is this done, that on the discharging of the cargo at its destined port, not more than 200 or 300 are found broken, out of 70 to 100,000 slates. The vessels (generally belonging to the place), are engaged by the different Slate Companies, as they require them—freights vary-ing, according to the state of supply and demand.

It may be interesting to the reader to know that this material is not only converted into roofing slates, but is also sawn into slabs by engines with circular saws, driven by water power. Some pieces are only sawn at the two ends, being left so that they may be again sawn and split at the places where they are to be sent to. Others are sawn all round, and planed on both sides if not of a good quality. Pieces of almost any dimensions are procurable, but the railway having so narrow a gauge, and its windings being so sharp and angular, those above 9 feet by 7 feet cannot be brought down to Portmadoc for shipment.

The numerous purposes to which these slabs are devoted is astonishing. They are extensively used as pavement, for the flooring of houses, warehouses, terraces, balconies, conserva-tories, &c., for steps, for the lining of damp walls, for wash-houses, and baths, powder magazines, larders, wine-cellars and dairies. They are also manufactured into cisterns, tanks, wine-coolers, bread pickling and pig-feeding troughs, urinals, filters, head and foot stones for graves, tombs and monuments, clock faces, and sun dials. Chimney pieces are largely made of slate, varying in price from six shillings to twenty five pounds. Mr. Samuel Holland has recently erected machinery for making school slates, at Rhiwbryfdir. But the latest and most wonderful process applied to slate is that of enamelling.— a species of glazing which shields the substance beneath, and enables it to receive the adornment of colour. The various kinds of marbles, porphyries, and other costly materials are thus faithfully and beautifully imitated at a fraction of the cost of the articles represented. The cheapness of the material, its strength arising from its lamellar structure, estimated at four times the strength of stone flags, its union of compactness, lightness, and durability, as compared with marble, are calculated to introduce it generally into ornamental and deco-rative works, and to insure a large and permanent demand from the public. The exact method of laying on the colour is not made public; but we understand that the "slate after being coloured is exposed for several days to a temperature of 300 to 500 fahrenheit, and the colours are rendered so permanent that wash-stand tops and other articles used in hotels for years have been scarcely injured by wear." "In respect also of its smooth and perfect surface, and fine texture, it is admirably adapted to various ornamental and useful purposes." The following objects are manufactured according to this process: chimney pieces, table tops, skirtings, side-boards, billiard tables, ornamental daises, monuments, mural tablets, altar tablets, sun-dials, clock faces, pedestals, baths, vases, chiffonieres, candelabra, &c. Who can say but that some novel inventions may soon again be made to extend the application of slate to purposes still more surprising.

Previous to 1830, the Welsh slate trade laboured under a very heavy duty—amounting in some instances to 50 per cent. But in that year, when a move was made in Parliament to get the duty on coals carried coastwise repealed, Mr. Archer, at the instance of Mr. Samuel Holland, Junior, and one or two others—seeing in this a good opportunity to get the imposition on slates sent coastwise also abrogated, succeeded in introducing slates into the Coals Bill, and thus obtained the remission of the slate duty. This gave a great stimulation to the Welsh slate trade, which in the Northern English Counties had to contend with the Westmoreland slates introduced through Preston—duty free—and immediately had the effect of increasing the trade of the Welsh quarries, and diminishing that of the Westmoreland quarries. The improved mode of transit introduced by the Railway Company has had a great, although partly an imperceptible, effect on the growth and prosperity of the Festiniog Quarries. The former mode of conveyance from the quarries by carts and waggons to the river side below Tanybwlch, and thence by boats down Traethbach to the vessels lying near Portmadoc was expensive and most annoying, occasioning a good deal of damage to the slates, as well as the quarry proprietors being only able to ship during the spring tides. Although the facilities offered by the railway were not at first generally availed of, yet they were so palpable that it soon superseded the former clumsy and vexatious mode of transit. Of late years, the bulk of the slates are brought down by it, and at one-fourth of the cost of the old means of conveyance.

Slate being an article generally dependent on the state of trade generally, is subject to frequent fluctuations in prices. But every year, seeing slates brought into more general use, and introduced into new markets, and the demand thus constantly increasing, a greater stability and independence is imparted to the trade. Railway enterprises, the growth of old and the creation of new towns have greatly helped to place it in a less dependent position. About 15 years ago, a greater scope was given to it, when slates began to be exported from Portmadoc to Hamburgh and to the Baltic. About 10,000 tons, or a fifth of the shipments, are now annually exported to foreign countries. Hamburgh continues to be the chief entrepôt of this branch of the trade. Slates are forwarded from there by means of rivers, canals, and railways, to the interior of the continent—to Prussia, Germany, and even to Austria. The chief buildings, ecclesiastical edifices, and railway stations in those countries are now almost universally roofed with the produce of the Festiniog and other North Wales Quarries. Some thousands of tons are also exported every year to the Baltic,—to Copenhagen, Maluro, Stettin, Stratsund, Dantzic, Pillaw, Konigsburgh, &c. Several cargoes to Rotterdam, Dunkerque, Calais, &c., and lately, a small craft of 35 tons burthen came twice to Portmadoc from Iceland, for cargoes of the Festiniog slates.

The discovery of gold in Australia, in 1851, beside its indirect effect on the slate trade by the impulse it gave to the business of this country, also communicated to it a direct impression by connecting it with the markets of our antipodes. Melbourne rose up like some enchanted city pictured by the fertility of eastern imagination. Streets were formed in every direction—the houses being roughly erected, and roofed with timber, &c. But it was soon discovered that a more suitable article than timber must be provided to withstand the scorching heat, and the violent impetuous falls of rain of the climate. Slate was imported, and found to be by far the best resistant to these inclemencies, being not only used for roofing, but also to line the sides of houses. In 1852, 1853, and 1854, large quantities were forwarded from Portmadoc to Melbourne, Geelong, &c., by way of Liverpool, where they were re-shipped into the Australian Liners. Enormous profits—in many instances 80 per cent, were pocketed. But this golden harvest leading to over-speculation, the markets were glutted, and prices consequently declined considerably, until the export of slates to this colony has dwindled down to an insignificant quantity. Slates are also forwarded through Liverpool to the United States, the East and West Indies, the colony of the Cape of Good Hope, California, &c.

The Festiniog slates received the encomiums of the jurors of Class I. of the great Exhibition of 1851, and to them were awarded the Prize Medal. The jurors remark: "These slates, which are of superior quality, are chiefly in use for covering buildings. They are also employed as walls for cisterns to hold Water; but in this case large slabs are required. Several such slabs are exhibited, some of which are more than 15 feet by 8 feet. Most of them are dressed to a rough polish, but one is in the state it came from the quarry. Dendritic markings may be observed on its surface. The jury have awarded a Prize Medal to Mr. John W. Greaves." (Reports of the juries, page 8). The jurors of Class 27 observe (page 555 of the Reports, &c.) "some beautiful specimens of slate flags from the quarries at Festiniog, North Wales, are worthy of Honourable Mention (awarded a Prize Medal by Class I.), and careful attention, as presenting a cheap and admirable pavement of great beauty, and in slabs so large as to prevent much chance of an irregular surface being produced, when much used. The flags are of fine quality, and have had a severe trial at the Transept Entrance of the building, where some millions of footsteps have hitherto failed in producing any mark of unequal wear."

Mr. Holland forwarded specimens of his slates to the Paris Exhibition, of 1854, and they were deemed worthy of Honourable Mention. There are great hopes entertained that the heavy preventive duty imposed on slates imported into France from this country will be repealed by the present wise and vigorous government of that country, and one of the best means of aiding the government of the Emperor to effect this was, we think, the forwarding of specimens of the superior article manufactured at Festiniog, to the Exhibition. There, also, it must have met the observation and scrutiny of gentlemen from the remotest parts of the European Continent, and no one can foretell what may be the beneficial influences that will follow from the publicity thus obtained. After the Exhibition (1851) orders were received from places, the names of which were not previously known in Portmadoc.

The following list will fully illustrate the progress of the Portmadoc slate trade:—

TONNAGE OF SLATES SHIPPED AT PORTMADOC
FROM 1825 TO 1855.

Years.	Tons.	Years.	Tons.	Years	Tons.	Years.	Tons.
1825	11396	1833	14383	1841	28845	1849	33960
1826	13136½	1834	15330	1842	22822	1850	44864
1827	10290	1835	17942	1843	24590	1851	46298
1828	9940	1836	20187	1844	36348	1852	46232
1829	10464½	1837	23272	1845	43832	1853	48851
1830	11035	1838	24566	1846	43761	1854	51109
1831	12287	1839	27204	1847	40451	1855	46802
1832	14561	1840	31200	1848	36750		

But we accept of this great increase only as a guarantee of future progress. We see new quarries opened in other districts. The extensive workings now carried on at Llanfihangel-y-penant, on the lands of G. A. Huddart, Esq., of Brynkir, and Richard Morris Griffith, Esq., Bangor, by the Isallt and Gor-seddau Companies bid fair to become the sources of great wealth not only to the district where they are situated, but also to Portmadoc, with which they will be in communication by the railway now in course of construction.

IMPORT TRADE.

Coals, limestones, and oats for seed were almost the only articles imported into the estuary of Traethmawr previous to the formation of the harbour of Portmadoc, and these in only insignificant quantities. But in 1824 a regular trade was established between this place and Liverpool, the first *regular* trader started for there being a small vessel built and placed upon the trade by Mr. Holland, Senior, in that year, and significantly called the "Experiment." Others were soon put on the station; but previous to this trader being established, the shopkeepers of the neighbourhood, and those at Maen-twrog, Festiniog, &c., received their supply of goods from Chester, by carriers, across the country, which mode of transit caused much delay, loss, and inconvenience. It would only be considered tedious to go at length into a minute history of the enlargement of this trade. We shall therefore merely supply the reader with some few facts that will enable him to form an opinion of its present state. The gross imports in 1855 amounted to—

30,000 feet of Timber:—Deal, Oak, and Birch pieces from British North America, and Oak roughly hewn for the purpose of Ship-building from Gloucester—the produce of the Forest of Dean, and from Southampton, Portsmouth, &c., the produce of the celebrated New Forest, Hampshire, &c.

4,000 tons of Coal and Culm, from the Lancashire and South Wales Coal Fields principally.

4000 tons of Limestones, from Plymouth, Cork, Limerick, Waterford, &c.

2,000 Sacks of Flour, and 200 Sacks of Bran, Beans, &c., from Liverpool.

200 quarters of Oats, Barley, &c., from different places.

300 tons of Grocery, from Liverpool, &c.

1,000 tons of sundry goods, Iron, Powder, Oil, &c., &c.

This trade is on the increase every year, and had the means of communication with other districts been of a more perfect character, it would have attained a still greater development. The uncertainty of the receipt of goods from Liverpool by the sailing traders now established, causes a good deal of mer-chandise to be forwarded from that town, Manchester, and other places to the district of Portmadoc by rail to Carnarvon, and from thence overland by carts, &c. In the summer of 1855 a steamer plied between Liverpool, Portmadoc and Aber-ystwith, It is to be hoped that it was a pioneer to a permanent line of steam communication, which is much required in lieu of the present uncertain, and in every way imperfect, means of transport.

SHIPBUILDING TRADE.

Ships were built in the estuaries of Traethmawr and Traethbach long anterior to the existence of this place. It is well known that several were built near Carreghylldrem, a bold swelling rock in the parish of Llanfrothen, overhanging the road from Beddgelert to Tanybwlch, and now about five miles inland. Towards the end of the last century a vessel of 300 tons burthen was built at Minffordd, distant half a mile from the Merionethshire end of the Embankment, on a spot which has since then been metamorphosed into a kitchen garden belong-ing to an old antiquated house called Rhos. Great many good-sized ones were launched at Tygwyn-y-gamlas, Abergafren, Borthwen, and Aberia, in the Traethbach. Borth y Gest was also a shipbuilding station since some centuries.

The first vessel made at Portmadoc was erected in 1824, and called the "Two Brothers," and by Mr. Henry Jones, who

continues to take the lead in this branch of industry. A small
number were made by him and others in the 15 years following,
but the business did not wear a very thriving appearance until
about the year 1840. Since that year it has enlarged in
amount, at an increased ratio every year, until at the present
time it employs as many as 100 carpenters, joiners, and
smiths, and turns out from £20,000 to £25,000 worth of shipping property annually.

Great improvements have been wrought in the shape of the
vessels built since so recent a period as thirty years ago. Short,
bluff-bowed, stout-sterned, and tublike vessels of a small size
were those in vogue then. Provided a vessel had a good stowage room, all was considered well, no regard being apparently
paid to her sailing qualities. But gradually a more easy wedge-
like overhanging shape was substituted for the bluff, perpendi-
cular bow, and a more gradual curvature was adopted for the
stern—greater length given—and altogether vessels were
modelled with greater regard to sailing and weatherly qualities
than heretofore—stowage not being deemed the only essential
quality constituting a good coasting vessel. And now, few
places can boast of such a handsome and substantially built
mercantile fleet as the one Portmadoc possesses, particularly
those vessels in it that were made during the last few years.
The class generally built here are those made to carry from I20
to 160 tons, none below 70 tons, and but few above 16o tons, this
range being found the most suitable one to meet the requirements of the slate trade. Occasionally, vessels of 300 burthen
have been launched for Liverpool firms to be employed in the
South American, Californian, and Australian trades. Several
ships have been lengthened here—most of them by putting a
new part in amidships. This has not only proved favourable to
their sailing powers, but profitable in the shape of larger dividends. The bulk of the timber used is imported from Southampton, Colchester, and Gloster. The remainder is obtained
from the country around, and is far preferable on account of
its superior hardness and toughness. There are six shipbuilders
now connected with the place, and this branch of trade bids
fair to become the source of increased prosperity, and commercial importance to it. Every year witnesses a greater number
of vessels laid down and launched, and the money consequently
circulated thus increasing, must find its way towards, and make
its effect felt on other classes of the population.

SHIPPING PROPERTY

This almost ranks as next to the slate trade in importance—its influencies ramifying through the whole community, and its interest bearing on the well-being and comfort of every class. Since its commencement thirty years ago, it has been gradually increasing until its estimated value at the present time approximates to the amount of £125,000, the greatest part of which is owned by the industrial and labouring classes, a fact we have great pleasure in noticing. The opening and increasing productiveness of the Festiniog Quarries created a demand for shipping to carry away their produce, and as every inducement and facility were offered for the building of vessels, and those already built returning such handsome profits (some of them as much as 25 per cent. annually on the capital invested, in years when trade was brisk), these causes combined to advance the tonnage and value of this property to what they are at present. About £25,000 is annually added to it, and it will, undoubtedly, be doubled in a few years hence. Though chiefly employed in conveying slates to English and foreign ports, a great part of its revenue is derived from *back* freight. Besides enriching the place by its returns, the expenditure of the shipping in repairing, provisioning, &c., is considerable—thus proving a resource in a double sense. In 1841, a Mutual Ship Insurance Society was established here through the aid of John W. Greaves, Esq., of Tanyrallt, and Samuel Holland, Esq., of Plasynpenrhyn,—the first society of the kind formed and carried out in North Wales, we believe. In this, Portmadoc has taken the lead of seaport towns of far higher pretensions. It has gone on most satisfactorily since its commencement—having been managed with singular ability and success. If a proof be needed of this, the following facts will fully supply it. Its premiums have not been above 2 per cent. yearly on an average, while from 5 to 7 per cent. is exacted by London and other offices. Property to the amount of £100,000 is now insured in it. It has been of very great benefit to the shipping interest, affording indemnification for sudden losses, thus giving a desirable stability to this property, which has had a marked effect on its progress. By this influence in increasing its means of communication, the commerce of the place has also been materially benefited. The society has extended its advantages to Pwllheli and Barmouth—vessels from these ports being insured by it on the same footing, and their owners allowed the same privileges as those of Portmadoc.

The penning of these remarks has been to their author verily a pleasant duty: it has recalled to his mind many interesting associations, and revived in his memory numerous scenes and events with which he was personally connected. He has seen Portmadoc when the greater part of its site was a wild waste covered with gorse, and when its size and population were not one tenth of what they are at the present time. He has watched it gradually progressing into a place of great impor- tance from its wealth and commercial activity. We are apt to lose sight of the means employed in the results accomplished— of the violence of the struggle in the glory of the victory. Thus with regard to Portmadoc; how few there are who can picture satisfactorily to their mind the enterprise, skill, endurance, and energy that were required to battle with natural difficulties of no ordinary character, and disappointments innumerable which the founder of this place, and his worthy coadjutor met with! and which finally conquered all obstacles, covering the "drowned lands" with verdure, rendering the unproductive wilderness a scene of beauty and fertility, and transforming the situation occupied by sand heaps into a thriving and prosperous seaport town. We have endeavoured, therefore, in this essay, not only to delineate the present state of Portmadoc, and those resour- ces on which its prosperity mainly depends, but also to exhibit the *history* of the improvements that have terminated so favourably. We have also felt it necessary to introduce some strictures on the sanitary condition of the place, and the apathy shewn by its inhabitants to the intellectual wants of the com- munity,—endeavouring to demonstrate how easily the one might be remedied, and the others supplied.

The prospects of Portmadoc are hopeful and highly satis- factory. There is every reason to believe that its size, popula- tion, and trade will be doubled in a few years hence. Indeed should the projects of establishing a communication with Liver- pool by steamer, and of uniting it with Carnarvon by a line of railway, be carried out—results of an astounding character will no doubt be witnessed here. The carrying out of these into effect, by providing a cheap, speedy, and regular means of transport would immensely add to, and augment the commerce, industry, and facilities of the place, and render it one of the most important towns in North Wales.